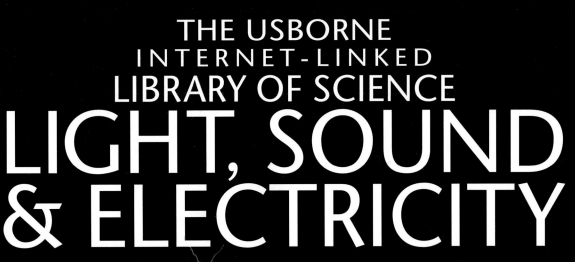

THE USBORNE
INTERNET-LINKED
LIBRARY OF SCIENCE
LIGHT, SOUND
& ELECTRICITY

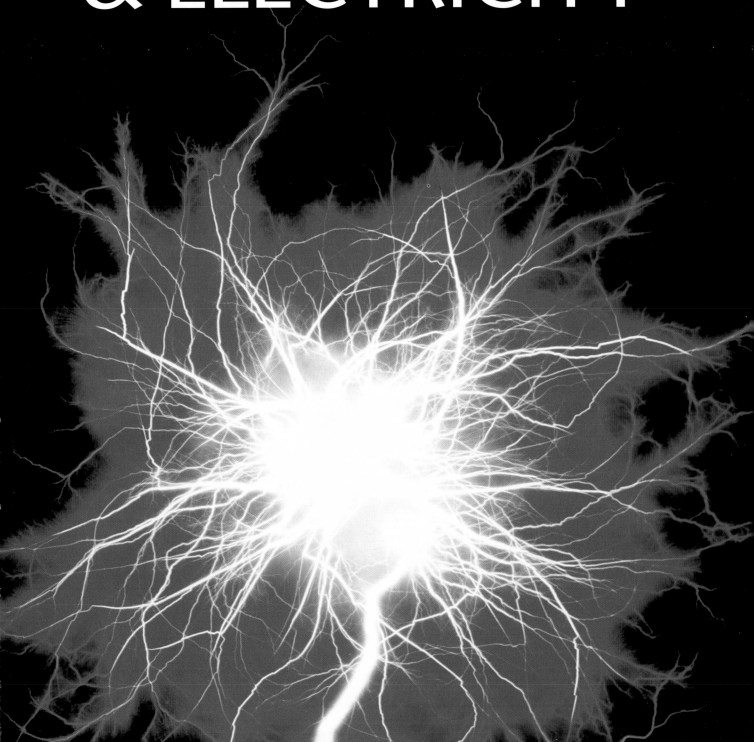

First published in 2001 by Usborne Publishing Ltd,
Usborne House, 83-85 Saffron Hill, London EC1N 8RT, England.

www.usborne.com

Printed in Spain

AE First published in America, 2002.

THE USBORNE
INTERNET-LINKED
LIBRARY OF SCIENCE
LIGHT, SOUND & ELECTRICITY

Kirsteen Rogers, Phillip Clarke, Alastair Smith
and Corinne Henderson

Designed by Karen Tomlins, Chloë Rafferty, Ruth Russell,
Candice Whatmore and Adam Constantine

Digital illustrations by Verinder Bhachu
Digital imagery by Joanne Kirkby

Edited by Laura Howell

Cover design: Nicola Butler

Consultant: Dr Tom Petersen

Web site adviser: Lisa Watts
Editorial assistant: Valerie Modd

Managing designer: Ruth Russell
Managing editor: Judy Tatchell

INTERNET LINKS

If you have access to the Internet, you can visit the Web sites we have recommended in this book. On every page, you will find descriptions of what is on each Web site, and why they are worth visiting. Here are some of the things you can do on the recommended sites in this book:

- see how a rainbow is formed
- take a virtual trip to the Sun and find out about its energy
- explore the amazing world of optical illusions
- try out interactive experiments on many different topics, such as wave behavior
- see and hear the different instruments in an orchestra
- experiment with interactive models of magnetic materials

USBORNE QUICKLINKS

To visit the recommended sites in this book, go to the Usborne Quicklinks Web site, where you'll find links you can click on to take you straight to the sites. Just go to *www.usborne-quicklinks.com* and follow the simple instructions you find there.

Sometimes, Web addresses change or sites close down. We regularly review the sites listed in Quicklinks and update the links if necessary. We will provide suitable alternatives at *www.usborne-quicklinks.com* whenever possible. Occasionally, you may get a message saying that a site is unavailable. This may be a temporary problem, so try again later.

DOWNLOADABLE PICTURES

Pictures marked with the symbol ★ may be downloaded for your own personal use, for example, for homework or for a project, but may not be used for any commercial or profit-related purpose. To find these pictures, go to Usborne Quicklinks and follow the instructions there.

USING THE INTERNET

You can access most of the Web sites described in this book with a standard home computer and a Web browser (this is the software that enables you to access Web sites and view them on your computer).

Some Web sites need extra programs, called plug-ins, to play sounds or to show videos or animations. If you go to a site and you don't have the right plug-in, a message saying so will come up on the screen. There is usually a button you can click on to download the plug-in. Alternatively, go to Usborne Quicklinks and click on Net Help, where you will find links to plug-ins.

INTERNET SAFETY

Here are three important guidelines to follow to keep you safe while you are using the Internet:

- If a Web site asks you to register or log in, ask permission from your parent or guardian before typing in any information.
- Never give out personal information, such as your home address or phone number.
- Never arrange to meet someone that you communicated with on the Internet.

www.usborne-quicklinks.com

Go to Usborne Quicklinks for:
- direct links to all the Web sites described in this book
- free downloadable pictures, which appear throughout this book marked with a ★ symbol

SEE FOR YOURSELF

The *See for yourself* boxes in this book contain experiments, activities or observations which we have tested. Some recommended Web sites also contain experiments, but we have not tested all of these. This book will be used by readers of different ages and abilities, so it is important that you do not tackle an experiment on your own, either from the book or the Web, that involves equipment that you do not normally use, such as a kitchen knife or stove. Instead, ask an adult to help you.

CONTENTS

These glowing threads are fiber-optic cables. Light is passed through them by thin, hair-like glass strands called optical fibers. Fiber-optic cables have many uses, from telecommunications to looking inside the human body.

LIGHT, SOUND AND ELECTRICITY

Light, sound and electricity are all forms of energy. Light and sound travel through substances as different types of waves. Electricity is a type of energy which can be easily converted into other forms. In this book, you can find out about all three types of energies, and see examples of modern technology which make use of them.

WAVES

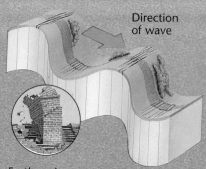

All **waves** carry energy. There are two main types of waves – mechanical and electromagnetic. **Mechanical waves**, including water waves and sound waves, are vibrations in a solid, liquid or gas. Electromagnetic waves, such as light waves and radio waves, are vibrations of a different kind. For more about these waves see pages 18-19.

Direction of wave

Earthquakes are waves that travel through rock. The vibrations can be strong enough to destroy buildings.

TRANSFERRING ENERGY

Any substance through which waves travel is called a **medium**. Water, glass and air are different types of medium. A mechanical wave carries energy through a medium by making its particles vibrate. Each vibrating particle makes its neighbor vibrate, so passing the energy through the substance.

As these droplets fall into the water, waves spread out in a circle, carrying energy away from the disturbed area.

Waves such as those shown in the pictures below are caused by the water's particles vibrating up and down. The particles don't travel onwards with the wave.

Like the water particles themselves, the bird isn't moved forward by the passing wave.

A wave does not permanently disturb the medium it travels through. Each particle gradually stops vibrating and settles in its original position.

The particles in a wave vibrate less as they lose energy, and the water becomes still.

The ripples on this pond are water waves. As they move away from the source of the disturbance they lose energy, and so become smaller.

TYPES OF WAVES

All waves can be described as either transverse or longitudinal, depending on the direction of their vibrations.

Transverse waves are waves in which the particles vibrate at right angles to the direction the wave is traveling. Water waves are transverse waves.

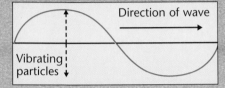

Particles in a transverse wave vibrate at right angles to the direction of the wave.

In **longitudinal waves**, the particles vibrate in the same direction as the wave is traveling. The particles of the medium vibrate forward and backward, acting like the coils in a spring as they are squeezed together and then spread out. Sound waves are longitudinal waves.

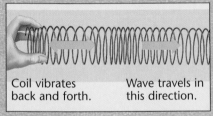

Coil vibrates back and forth.   Wave travels in this direction.

The coils in this moving spring show how longitudinal waves travel.

MEASURING WAVES

Transverse waves create a regular pattern of high points, called **peaks**, and low points, called **troughs**. A complete wave is known as a **cycle**. It has one peak and one trough.

The number of complete waves that pass a point in one second is called the **frequency**. This is measured in **hertz** (**Hz**), named after the German scientist, Heinrich Hertz (1857-1894), who was the first person to discover and use radio waves.

The distance between a point on one wave and the same point on the next, for example, between two troughs, is called the **wavelength**.

The height from a particle's rest position to a peak is called **amplitude**. This becomes less as a wave moves away from its source and loses energy.

A wave is measured by its frequency, wavelength and amplitude.

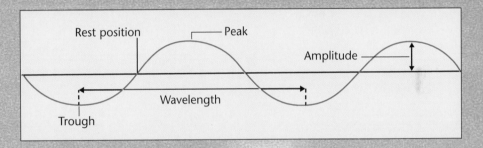

See for yourself

You can use this experiment to see the form of a transverse wave. Tie one end of a piece of string to a fixed point, such as a door knob, hold the other end and give it a sharp shake. You will see the form of the wave moving along the string. The string vibrates at right angles to the direction of the wave.

The string vibrates up and down.

The transverse wave travels in this direction.

Internet links

• Go to **www.usborne-quicklinks.com** for a link to **The Evergreen Project Web site** where you can read an easy-to-understand explanation of waves.

• Go to **www.usborne-quicklinks.com** for a link to the **BrainPop Web site** to watch a friendly movie on waves.

• Go to **www.usborne-quicklinks.com** for a link to the **PBS Savage Earth Web site** to see animations of movement along fault lines and a movie showing the after-effects of an earthquake in an urban area.

• Go to **www.usborne-quicklinks.com** for a link to the **Geology Labs On-line Web site** to become a virtual seismologist.

• Go to **www.usborne-quicklinks.com** for a link to the **Physics 2000 Web site** to learn about electromagnetic waves through a variety of activities.

• Go to **www.usborne-quicklinks.com** for a link to the **Physics Department Web site** for an in-depth introduction to waves and some interactive wave activities.

• Go to **www.usborne-quicklinks.com** for a link to the **Waves Web pages** to find out about various aspects of wave behavior and watch wave animations.

• Go to **www.usborne-quicklinks.com** for a link to the **The Sea Web site** for a concise definition of waves.

WAVE BEHAVIOR

When a wave hits an obstacle, or passes from one substance (medium) to another, it can change in speed, direction or shape. Before the change, the wave is called the **incident wave**. The examples on these pages show water waves, but all waves behave in the same way.

Tsunami are giant waves that slow down and rapidly increase in height as they enter shallow water.

REFLECTION

When an incident wave hits an obstacle, for example when a water wave hits a sea wall, it bounces back. This is called **reflection**. The wave is reflected back at an angle equal to its angle of approach. It is then called a **reflected wave**.

The shape of a reflected wave depends both on the shape of the incident wave and the shape of the obstacle it hits. The diagrams below show what happens when straight and curved incident waves hit differently shaped obstacles.

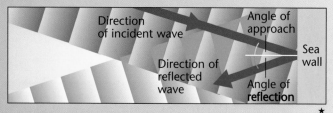

Direction of incident wave

Angle of approach

Direction of reflected wave

Sea wall

Angle of reflection

★

The angle of reflection of a wave is the same as the angle of approach of the incident wave.

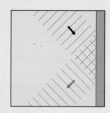

Straight waves hitting a straight barrier produce straight reflected waves.

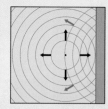

Circular waves hitting a straight barrier produce circular reflected waves.

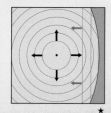

★

Circular waves hitting an inward-curving barrier produce straight reflected waves.

Waves at sea are relatively straight. As they approach the shallow waters of a beach, they bend until they match the curves of its shoreline. This is an example of refraction.

REFRACTION

When an incident wave enters a new medium it changes speed. Its wavelength* changes, but its frequency* doesn't. In the diagram below, the waves slow down in the new medium. Their wavelength gets shorter, but the number of peaks passing in a second (the frequency) stays the same.

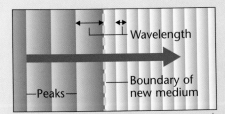

Waves change speed as they enter a new medium. ★

If a wave enters a new medium at an angle, it changes both speed and direction. This is called **refraction**. A wave that has undergone refraction is called a **refracted wave**.

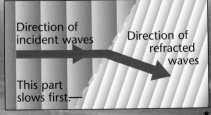

Waves change speed and direction as they enter a new medium at an angle. ★

Deep and shallow water act as different substances. The first part of the wave to enter the shallows slows down before the rest of the wave. This changes the wave's direction.

INTERFERENCE

If two or more waves meet, they have an effect on each other. This effect is called **interference**. The kind of interference depends on which parts of the waves coincide.

If two peaks of the same amplitude* arrive in the same place at the same time, they combine to form a peak twice as large. This is an example of **constructive interference**.

 + =

If a peak meets a trough of the same size, they cancel each other out and the wave disappears. This is an example of **destructive interference**.

 + =

See for yourself

To see wave interference, hold a small pebble in each hand and drop them, at the same time, into a bath filled with water. The ripples made by the pebbles will move out in circles. Where they cross each other you might see, very briefly, both constructive and destructive interference.

Constructive interference

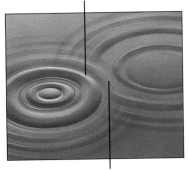

Destructive interference

DIFFRACTION

When an incident wave passes through a gap, it spreads out and bends. This is an example of **diffraction**. The smaller the gap compared to the wavelength of the wave, the more it is diffracted.

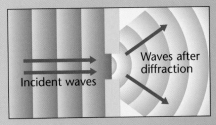

A wave passing through a gap smaller than its wavelength is diffracted a lot.

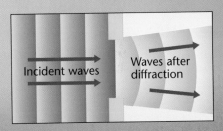

A wave passing through a gap larger than its wavelength is hardly diffracted at all.

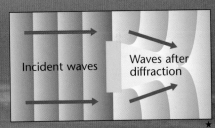

Waves can also be diffracted when striking the edge of an obstacle. ★

Internet links

• Go to **www.usborne-quicklinks.com** for a link to the **NASA Observatorium Web site** to find out about tsunami.

• Go to **www.usborne-quicklinks.com** for a link to the **Physics 2000 Web site** to perform interactive wave experiments.

• Go to **www.usborne-quicklinks.com** for a link to the **Britannica Encyclopedia Web site** to read an in-depth definition of the term "refraction" and follow the links for helpful diagrams and pictures.

• Go to **www.usborne-quicklinks.com** for a link to the **ExploreScience Web site** for an interactive demonstration of wave interference.

Amplitude, Frequency, Wavelength, 9.

SOUND

Sound is a form of energy carried by waves of vibrating particles. These waves, called **sound waves**, can travel through solids, liquids and gases, but they cannot travel through a vacuum as there are no particles of any sort to vibrate. For this reason, sound cannot travel out in space.

The sound of falling leaves measures 10dB.

SOUND WAVES

Sound waves are longitudinal waves. This means that the particles vibrate in the same direction as the wave travels.

For instance, inside a loudspeaker a paper cone vibrates forward and backward, sending sound energy into the air. As the cone moves forward, it presses together air particles in front of it. As it moves backward, it leaves an area where the particles are more spaced out.

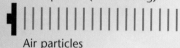
Cone of loudspeaker (not moving)

Air particles

Cone moves forward.

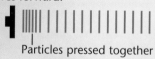
Particles pressed together

Cone moves backward.

Particles spread out

See for yourself

You can feel sound vibrations with a balloon and a radio. Turn on a radio and hold a balloon about 4in away from the speaker. The vibrations of the sounds make the air in the balloon vibrate.

Sound waves can be shown as a wavy line. The peaks show where particles have been squashed. The troughs show where particles are spread out. Wave diagrams show the number of waves per second (frequency) and their strength (amplitude).

Diagram showing sound waves

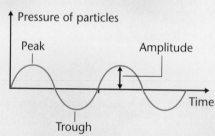

Wave frequency is measured in hertz (Hz). Sound waves with frequencies between about 20 and 20,000 hertz can be heard by the human ear and are commonly described as sound. Sound waves below this range are known as **infrasound**, and above it are **ultrasound**.

High sounds, such as birdsong, have high-frequency waves.

Low sounds, such as the rumble made by the engine of a heavy truck, have low-frequency waves.

LOUDNESS

Loud sounds are waves with a large amplitude. Soft sounds are waves with a small amplitude. As a sound travels further away from its source, the amplitude becomes smaller and so the sound becomes quieter.

The loudness of sound is measured in **decibels** (**dB**). The blue whale is the loudest animal in the world. It makes sounds of up to 188dB.

Aircraft make such loud sounds that ground crew wear ear protectors to avoid hearing damage.

SPEED OF SOUND

Sound waves travel at different speeds in different substances. They travel more quickly in solids than in liquids, and more quickly in liquids than in gases.

The speed of sound waves as they travel through dry air at 0°C is 331 meters per second. This speed increases if the air temperature goes up, and decreases if the temperature of the air goes down.

A speed that is faster than the speed of sound in the same conditions is known as a **supersonic speed**. One that is slower is a **subsonic speed**.

As it reaches supersonic speed, an aircraft makes a deafening bang called a **sonic boom**. In this photo, the sound waves can be seen as they disturb the misty air.

The sound of an aircraft landing measures about 120dB.

ECHOES

Echoes are sound waves that have reflected (bounced) off a surface and are heard shortly after the original sound. Echoes can be used to find the position of objects. This is done by timing how long the echoes take to return to their source.

Ultrasonic sound waves are most often used because waves of high frequency bend less around obstacles in their path. The waves spread out less than ordinary sound waves and give more accurate information about the surface reflecting them.

When animals such as bats and dolphins use echoes, it is called **echo location**. They use it to find their way around or to locate prey.

Sonar is the name given to the method used by ships to measure the depth of sea water, or to detect underwater objects, such as shipwrecks or schools of fish. The echoes are detected by equipment on board the ship.

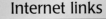

Ultrasound waves sent from the ship bounce off the wreck. A computer times the echoes to find the wreck's position.

Dolphins send out streams of over 700 ultrasonic clicks in a second. The time the echoes take to return can tell them how far away they are from schools of fish.

Echoes are also used in **ultrasound scanning** to see inside the body – for example to check on the growth of an unborn baby inside its mother. Bone, muscle and fat all reflect ultrasonic waves differently. A computer uses this information to make a picture.

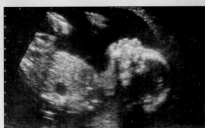

Ultrasound scan of an unborn baby

Internet links

• Go to www.usborne-quicklinks.com for a link to the **BrainPop Web site** to watch a friendly movie about sound.

• Go to www.usborne-quicklinks.com for a link to the **Submarines, Secrets and Spies Web site** to take a sound quiz.

• Go to www.usborne-quicklinks.com for a link to the **How Stuff Works Web site** to find out why sonic booms occur.

• Go to www.usborne-quicklinks.com for a link to **The Organization for Bat Conservation Web site** to learn how bats use echo location.

MUSICAL INSTRUMENTS

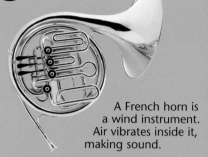

Musical instruments work by making sound waves. The shape and size of the instrument and the material of which it is made affect the sound. Some instruments have a soundbox that **resonates**. This means that it vibrates at the same frequency as the air vibrations created by the original sound, making the sound fuller and richer.

A French horn is a wind instrument. Air vibrates inside it, making sound.

TYPES OF INSTRUMENTS

Musical instruments can be divided into groups depending on the way they make sounds. **Stringed instruments**, such as harps and violins, have stretched strings that vibrate when you pluck or slide a bow across them. The strings inside a piano vibrate when they are hit by felt-covered hammers controlled by the keys. The more the strings vibrate, the louder the sound.

The bridge of this violin carries vibrations from the strings into the body of the instrument (its soundbox).

The bow strings are made of horsehairs. They slide across the strings, making them vibrate.

The soundbox resonates, making the sound fuller and louder.

Wind instruments work by making a column of air vibrate inside them. The vibrations are produced in different ways. For example in a trumpet, the player's lips vibrate in a cup-shaped mouthpiece. This sound is then made louder, or **amplified**, by the tube and the flared end of the instrument.

Early trumpets had long, straight tubes. In modern trumpets like this one, the tube is coiled, making it easier to hold.

Clarinets and oboes have a mouthpiece that contains one or two pieces of reed. These vibrate as air is blown past them.

Percussion instruments produce sound when they are beaten, scraped or shaken. A drum, for example, has a tight skin which you beat with your hand or a stick. The vibrations make the air inside the drum vibrate, and the hollow shape of the drum amplifies the sound.

The vibrations of a drum skin resonate inside the drum and are amplified.

ELECTRIC INSTRUMENTS

In **electric instruments**, such as an electric guitar, small sound vibrations produced by the strings are amplified by an electronic amplifier instead of a soundbox. Special effects, such as echoes, can also be added electronically to the sound.

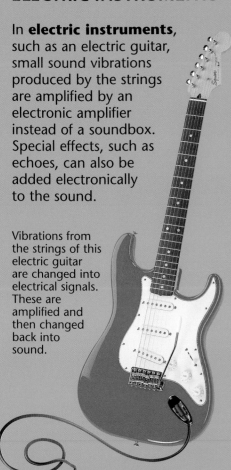

Vibrations from the strings of this electric guitar are changed into electrical signals. These are amplified and then changed back into sound.

SYNTHESIZED SOUND

A **sound synthesizer** is an instrument that stores sound waves as binary code* in its electronic memory. The synthesizer can reproduce a sound by converting the code for the sound into an electric current and sending it to a loudspeaker.

The sounds of musical instruments, as well as other noises, such as dogs barking, can be stored as binary code and reproduced by a synthesizer.

This keyboard synthesizer contains binary code for the sound waves of many different instruments.

* Binary code, 44; Hertz, 9.

PITCH

The highness or lowness of a sound is known as its **pitch**. Sound waves with a high frequency produce sounds of a high pitch, those with a low frequency, a low pitch. Musical sounds of a specific pitch are called **notes**. For example, the note known as **Middle C**, which is the C nearest to the middle of a piano keyboard, has a frequency of about 262 hertz*. The next C above it has a higher frequency – about 523 hertz.

The size of an instrument affects the pitch of the notes that can be played on it. For example, in a stringed instrument, the longer the string, the lower the pitch. This is why a double bass makes lower notes than a violin.

A harp has strings that vibrate as they are plucked. Strings of different lengths make notes of different pitches.

Players can change the pitch of the sounds an instrument makes. For example, a guitar or violin player presses down on the strings. This shortens the length of string that can vibrate, and so it makes higher notes. On a flute or recorder, the player covers and uncovers holes. This alters the length of the column of air that can vibrate inside it, and so changes the notes produced.

Pressing the keys on this flute covers the holes. This lengthens the air column, and so lowers the pitch of the note.

HARMONICS

Most instruments produce complex sound waves that have higher, quieter sounds mixed in. These sounds are called **harmonics**. They give an instrument its individual sound quality, or **timbre**.

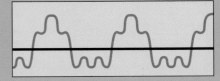

On a sound wave diagram, harmonics look like extra little waves. This diagram shows the waves made by an instrument.

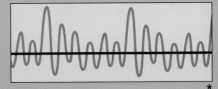

These are the sound waves of the same note played by a different instrument.

See for yourself

Try blowing across the top of an open, empty bottle. If you get it right, you will make the air column inside the bottle vibrate, producing a musical note. Now pour some water into the bottle and blow again. The water will have reduced the size of the air column, so the note that you produce will be higher.

Internet links

• Go to **www.usborne-quicklinks.com** for a link to the **Data Dragon Web site** to listen to a variety of musical instruments.

• Go to **www.usborne-quicklinks.com** for a link to the **Energy in the Air Web site** to hear the different instruments in an orchestra and find out more about sound.

• Go to **www.usborne-quicklinks.com** for links to the **Lemelson Center Web site** and the **How Stuff Works Web site** to find out how different guitars work.

• Go to **www.usborne-quicklinks.com** for links to the **Stomp Web pages** where you can find activities and information related to sound and percussion.

SOUND REPRODUCTION

By changing sound energy into electrical energy, sounds can be recorded and stored, to be played back at another time. In this form, sounds can also be sent over long distances, for example, over the Internet.

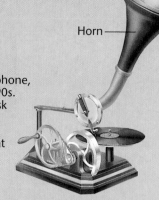

Horn

An early gramophone, made in the 1890s. Grooves on a disk made a needle vibrate, creating sound waves that were amplified (made louder) by the horn.

MICROPHONES

Sounds can be converted into an electric current by a device called a **microphone**. This contains a thin metal disk called a **diaphragm**, which is attached to an electromagnet*, that is, a coil of wire and a ring-shaped magnet.

When sound waves hit the diaphragm, it vibrates at the same frequency* as the waves. The diaphragm makes the wire coil vibrate. When the coil moves near the magnet, it creates an electric current which flows along the wire. The current produced varies according to the size and frequency of the sound waves.

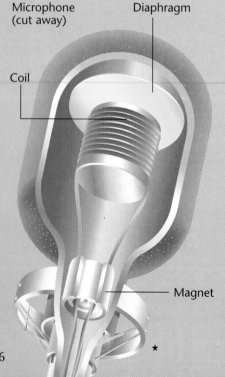

Microphone (cut away)

Diaphragm

Coil

Magnet

LOUDSPEAKERS

A **loudspeaker** turns an electric current from a source such as a microphone back into sound waves. Inside the loudspeaker there is an electromagnet. When an electric current flows through the coil in the electromagnet, it becomes magnetic. The coil is attached to a cone-shaped paper diaphragm.

The parts that make up a loudspeaker

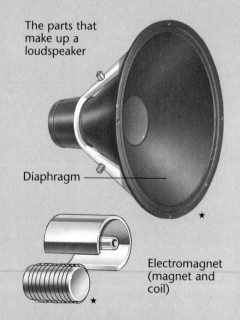

Diaphragm

Electromagnet (magnet and coil)

When a varying current produced from a sound wave flows through the coil, the force between the coil's magnetic field and that of the magnet makes both the coil and the diaphragm vibrate.

The air in front of the diaphragm vibrates to create sound waves of the same frequency as the original sound.

CASSETTE RECORDERS

In a **cassette recorder**, sounds are recorded as a pattern of magnetized particles of iron or chromium oxide on plastic tape.

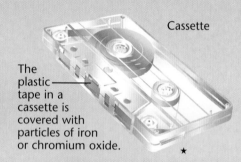

Cassette

The plastic tape in a cassette is covered with particles of iron or chromium oxide.

This is done by a part called the **recording head**, which is an electromagnet. A varying current produced from a sound wave passes from a microphone through a metal coil in the recording head. This causes variations in the head's magnetic field which arrange the metal particles on the tape into different patterns.

Recording head on cassette recorder

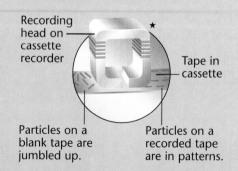

Tape in cassette

Particles on a blank tape are jumbled up.

Particles on a recorded tape are in patterns.

The patterns of particles on the tape can be read by a part called the **playback head**. It produces a varying current which is converted back into sound by a loudspeaker.

Electromagnet, 39; Frequency, 9.

ANALOG RECORDING

The varying current from a microphone produces a varying pattern of magnetic particles on a cassette tape. This is a continuous record of the position of the microphone's diaphragm as it vibrates back and forth in response to the sound waves, and is an example of **analog recording**.

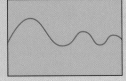

Original sound wave

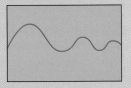

Recorded analog sound wave

One problem with analog recordings is that they can be changed by repeated use. For example, the playback heads on a cassette recorder gradually wear away the magnetic particles on the tape. This means that the sound heard becomes less like the original sound that was recorded.

See for yourself

You can hear the effect of magnetism on tape if you record something on a blank cassette. Wind the tape back to the start and take the cassette out of the machine. Unravel part of the tape and run a magnet over it a few times. Wind the tape back into the cassette and play it back. You will find that the magnet has rearranged the particles on the tape and has distorted the sound.

DIGITAL RECORDING

In **digital recording**, an electric current representing a sound is described by a code made up of the numbers 0 and 1 (binary code*). This is done by measuring the current at different points, a process called **sampling**.

The more points that are sampled, the closer to the original sound the recording is when played back. For example, in CD recording, 44,100 samples are taken every second. This produces a **high-fidelity recording** – one that sounds very similar to the original.

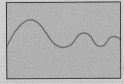

Analog sound wave

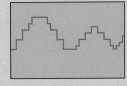

Low-fidelity digital sound wave

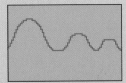

High-fidelity digital sound wave

With a digital recording, the same series of numbers is used to make up the sound each time it is played back. This means that it always sounds the same as when it was first recorded and is known as **perfect sound reproduction**.

Digitally recorded information can be stored as a file on computer. It can then be used in many ways, for example it can be transferred onto a CD, or sent across the Internet.

COMPACT DISCS

A **compact disc**, or **CD**, uses digital methods to store sound or other information. The binary code is represented by tiny **bumps**, and flat areas called **land**, on the surface of the disc.

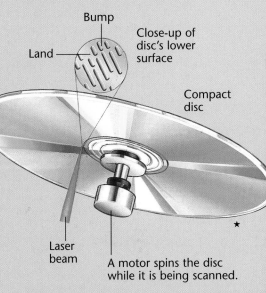

Bump

Land

Close-up of disc's lower surface

Compact disc

Laser beam

A motor spins the disc while it is being scanned.

Inside a CD player, a laser beam scans the disc's shiny underside. Light that hits land is reflected back to a light-sensitive detector, producing a pulse of current which is read as a binary 1. Light that hits a bump is scattered and produces no pulse, so it is read as a 0. The stream of digital pulses is converted to sound by a loudspeaker.

Internet links

• Go to **www.usborne-quicklinks.com** for links to the **How Stuff Works Web Pages,** the **BrainPop Web site** and the **Florida State University Web site** to find out how CDs, CD players, tape recorders and DVDs work.

• Go to **www.usborne-quicklinks.com** for a link to the **How Stuff Works Web site** to see animations showing how analog and digital recordings are made.

• Go to **www.usborne-quicklinks.com** for a link to the **PBS Newton's Apple Web site** where the technology of vinyl records is compared with that of CDs.

• Go to **www.usborne-quicklinks.com** for a link to the **Florida State University Web site** to watch an amazing animation showing how a speaker works.

*Binary code, 44.

ELECTROMAGNETIC WAVES

Electromagnetic waves are transverse waves* made up of continually changing electric and magnetic fields. Like mechanical waves, electromagnetic waves can travel through most solids, liquids and gases. They can also travel through a **vacuum** – an empty space where there are no particles of air or any other matter. All electromagnetic waves are invisible, except for those that make up light.

ELECTROMAGNETIC SPECTRUM

The complete range of electromagnetic waves, arranged in order of their wavelength* and frequency*, is known as the **electromagnetic spectrum**. At one end are waves with a short wavelength and high frequency, and at the other are waves with a long wavelength and low frequency. They all travel at the same speed – approximately 300,000 kilometers per second. This is known as the **speed of light**.

GAMMA RAYS

Gamma rays are short, high-frequency waves. They can kill living cells and are used to sterilize medical equipment by destroying any germs on them.

Gamma rays are used to keep these forceps free of germs.

X-RAYS

X-rays can travel through most soft substances but not hard, dense ones. X-rays are used in hospitals to make shadow pictures of parts of the body. They travel through soft tissue, such as skin and muscle, but not through hard bone. X-rays are also used for security at airports to check what may be hidden in people's luggage.

X-rays were used to create this image of a woman's foot in a shoe. The bones and metal shoe parts show up most clearly because the X-rays could not pass through them.

The electromagnetic spectrum

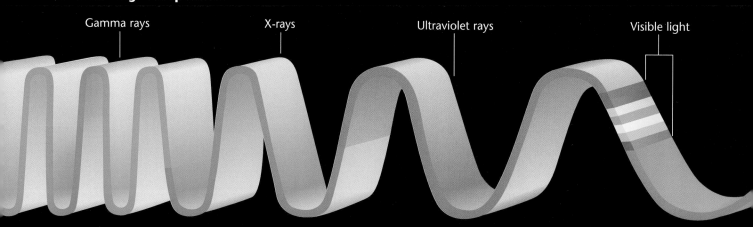

Gamma rays　　X-rays　　Ultraviolet rays　　Visible light

Short wavelength
High frequency

* Frequency, Transverse waves, Wavelength, 9.

UV RAYS

Ultraviolet (UV) rays have more energy than visible light (see below) and can cause chemical reactions to take place.

Sunscreen protects skin by blocking out harmful UV rays.

For example, UV rays from the Sun cause the skin to increase its production of a brown chemical called **melanin**. This makes the skin tanned. Too much exposure to UV rays can result in high levels of melanin, and may lead to skin cancer.

VISIBLE LIGHT

There is a narrow section of the electromagnetic spectrum that humans can see. This is called the **visible light spectrum**. You can find out more about visible light and the way it behaves on pages 20-23.

INFRARED RAYS

Infrared rays are given out by anything hot. For example, heat from the Sun travels to the Earth as infrared rays.

RADIO WAVES

Radio waves are those with the longest wavelength and lowest frequency. You can read more about them on page 32.

Microwaves are radio waves with a relatively short wavelength. They are easy to control and direct, and have many different uses.

In an ordinary oven, heat is passed from molecules at the edge of the food to ones in the middle. Microwave ovens work by making all the molecules in a food substance vibrate at the same time. This heats and cooks the food more quickly.

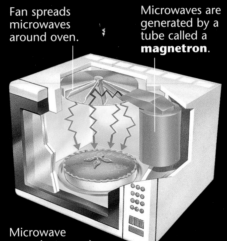

Fan spreads microwaves around oven.

Microwaves are generated by a tube called a **magnetron**.

Microwave oven (cut away)

RADAR

Radar (which stands for **ra**dio **d**etection **a**nd **r**anging) uses microwaves to find the position of distant objects, such as ships and aircraft. A transmitter sends out a beam of microwaves that is reflected off a solid object and picked up again by a receiver. This information is transformed into a screen image that shows the distance and direction of the object.

Radio telescope dishes like this one can pick up microwaves that travel from distant stars and planets. They can detect things that are too dark or too far away to be seen with normal telescopes.

Internet links

• Go to **www.usborne-quicklinks.com** for links to the **Imagers Web site**, the **Electromagnetic Spectrum Web pages** and the **Gondar Design Web site** for everything you ever wanted to know about electromagnetic waves.

• Go to **www.usborne-quicklinks.com** for a link to the **Physics 2000 Web site** where you can use a virtual X-ray machine.

• Go to **www.usborne-quicklinks.com** for a link to the **Infrared Astronomy Web site** to discover the history and science of infrared light and its uses.

• Go to **www.usborne-quicklinks.com** for a link to the **MicroWorlds Web site** to find out how and why scientists use the Advanced Light Source - a tool the size of a football field - to learn about structures as tiny as atoms and molecules.

Infrared rays

Radio waves

Microwaves

Waves used for standard radio and television broadcasting

Radio waves have the lowest frequency and longest wavelength. Gamma rays have the highest frequency and shortest wavelength.

Long wavelength
Low frequency

LIGHT AND SHADOW

Light is a form of energy. It is made up of electromagnetic waves which are part of the electromagnetic spectrum*. This part is known as **visible light** because it can be seen.

The beacon in this lighthouse rotates, flashing with intense bright light that can reach ships many miles out at sea.

LIGHT

Light waves are a type of transverse wave*. Like other waves, they transport energy from a source to its surroundings.

Any object that gives off light, for example the Sun or a light bulb, is said to be **luminous**. Most objects are non-luminous and can be seen only because they are reflecting the light from something luminous. For example, the Moon can only be seen when light from the Sun bounces off it.

Light from the Sun reflects off the surface of the Moon, enabling it to be seen.

Some luminous objects give off more light than others. The level of brightness is called **intensity**. The further you are from a source of light, the less intense the light is. This is because light waves spread out as they travel away from the source.

The bright flashlight gives more intense light than the small candle.

The light fades as the vibrations of the light waves become gradually smaller.

SHADOWS

Different types of substances allow different amounts of light to pass through them. Substances through which light can pass fully, such as clear glass, are said to be **transparent**. Substances which only let some light through are **translucent**. Frosted glass is translucent.

When light shines on an **opaque** object, the waves cannot pass through, so a dark area, called a **shadow**, forms on the other side.

Light

Light cannot pass through this ball, so a shadow is formed.

Opaque objects cast two types of shadow. If no light reaches an area, a dark shadow, called an **umbra**, is formed. If some light reaches an area, gray shadow is formed. This is called a **penumbra**, and it forms around the edge of the umbra. The smaller the light source, the more umbra and less penumbra it creates.

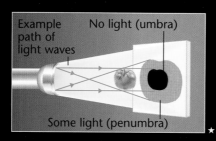

Example path of light waves

No light (umbra)

Some light (penumbra)

See for yourself

To see the two different kinds of shadow, hold a book over a piece of white paper under the light of a lamp. Notice the types of shadow it casts. If you move the book closer to the paper, you will see more umbra and less penumbra.

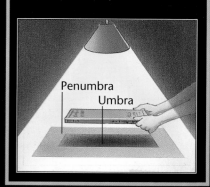

Penumbra
Umbra

* Electromagnetic spectrum, 18-19; Transverse waves, 9.

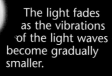

LASERS

Visible light is made up of several colors of different wavelengths* and frequencies*. Machines called **lasers** create beams of intense, pure color of one wavelength and frequency.

In a simple laser, a ruby rod absorbs light energy from a bright lamp. Atoms in the ruby gain the energy and give off bursts of light of a certain wavelength and frequency. Each burst of light causes other atoms in the ruby to give off light waves of the exact same type. Together they form a **laser beam**.

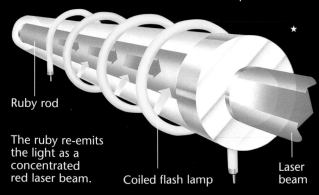

In this laser, a rod of ruby absorbs light from a coiled flash lamp.

★

Ruby rod

The ruby re-emits the light as a concentrated red laser beam.

Coiled flash lamp

Laser beam

The waves in a laser beam are **coherent**. This means that they travel in step with each other as everything about them is exactly the same. They stay together in a narrow, concentrated beam, making them easy to direct.

Some powerful lasers produce extremely hot beams of infrared light*. These are used in industry for melting through metals, diamonds and other tough materials. Less powerful lasers are used in certain types of eye surgery, such as replacing a detached retina. The laser makes a small heat scar which welds the detached part back into place.

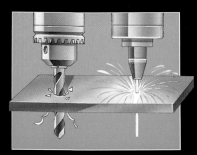

The drill (far left) makes a rough hole in the metal and produces waste shavings.

The powerful laser beam, by contrast, melts a clean hole.

FLUORESCENCE

Some substances can absorb energy, such as electricity or ultraviolet (UV) rays*, and give it out as light. They are described as **fluorescent** substances. They are widely used in advertising and paints as they make colors seem to glow.

This T-shirt has been washed with a washing powder containing fluorescent substances that absorb UV rays from the Sun and make white clothes look whiter.

Fluorescent lights consist of a tube filled with a gas such as neon. When electricity is passed through the tube, it gives energy to particles in the gas, which give off their new energy as light. Fluorescent lights give off different colors, depending on the gas used.

These colored lights are filled with fluorescent gases.

Internet links

• Go to www.usborne-quicklinks.com for a link to the **Center for Science Education Web site** to take a "Light Tour".

• Go to www.usborne-quicklinks.com for a link to the **Sun Block 99 Web site** where you can take a virtual trip to the Sun.

• Go to www.usborne-quicklinks.com for a link to the **Physics 2000 Web site** to find out all about lasers.

• Go to www.usborne-quicklinks.com for a link to the **Light! Web site** to learn about the history and science of light.

• Go to www.usborne-quicklinks.com for a link to the **How Stuff Works Web site** to discover more about light.

• Go to www.usborne-quicklinks.com for a link to the **Royal Holographic Gallery Web site** for amazing 3D images.

* Frequency, 9; Infrared rays, UV rays, 19; Wavelength, 9.

COLOR

Visible light appears colorless. It is also known as **white light**. In fact, it is made up of seven different colors: red, orange, yellow, green, blue, indigo and violet. Each color has a different wavelength* and frequency*. Together they make up the **visible light spectrum**. Colors of the spectrum are called **chromatic colors**.

DISPERSION

In 1666, scientist Isaac Newton discovered that white light could be divided into separate colors. This process is called **dispersion**. He dispersed light using a **prism** – a transparent solid with two flat surfaces at an angle to each other.

The picture below shows a prism. As light hits the first surface, the colors in it are bent (refracted*) by various amounts. This splits up the light into its separate colors. This dispersed light is refracted further when it hits the second surface. Colors with the shortest wavelengths, namely blue and violet, are refracted the most.

A rainbow is a result of dispersion that happens naturally. Water particles in the air act like prisms, separating sunlight into colors.

Rays of white light are separated into seven colors as they shine through this glass prism.

COLOR OF THE SKY

The color of the sky is a result of sunlight being scattered by small particles in the atmosphere. They reflect and diffract* sunlight, scattering high-frequency light waves, such as blue, most of all. When you look up at the sky, it appears blue because some of this scattered blue light reaches your eyes.

The different colors of this evening sky are caused by light scattering.

At sunrise and sunset, the light has to travel through more of the atmosphere before reaching your eyes. This means that the blue is scattered out before you can see it, leaving the sky with an orange or red glow. These are the colors of light with the lowest frequencies.

MIXING LIGHT

Almost any color of light can be made by **additive mixing**, that is, by using different combinations of red, green and blue light. For this reason red, green and blue are known as the **primary colors** of light.

Red, blue and green are the primary colors of light.

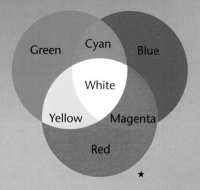

Cyan, magenta and yellow are the secondary colors of light.

When two primary colors are added together, the color they make is called a **secondary color**. Any two colors that can be added together to make white light, for example, red and cyan (opposite each other in the diagram above) are called **complementary colors**.

Diffraction, 11; Frequency, 9; Refraction, 11; Wavelength, 9.

SEEING IN COLOR

You can see colors when light reflecting off objects is detected by color-sensitive cells in your eyes.

All colored objects and paints contain **pigments**. These are substances that absorb certain colors and reflect others. You can see the color of an object because it reflects only light of that color. For example, a red flower reflects red light and absorbs all the other colors of the spectrum.

This bottle looks blue because it reflects only blue light and absorbs all the other colors.

White objects appear white because they reflect all the colors of light equally. Black objects absorb all the colors, so hardly any light is reflected, making the object look black. Black and white are known as **achromatic colors**.

The white feathers on this penguin reflect all the light that hits them.

The black feathers absorb all the light that hits them.

MIXING PIGMENTS

Pigments mix by a process called **subtractive mixing**. For example, the pigment in yellow paint absorbs blue light and the pigment in cyan paint absorbs red light. So when you mix yellow and cyan paints, the mixture can only reflect green light, making it look green. The primary colors of pigments are cyan, yellow and magenta. Red, blue and green are the secondary colors.

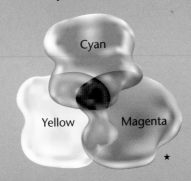

Cyan

Yellow   Magenta

Yellow and cyan pigments mix to make green because they absorb blue and red light.

See for yourself

You can see the colors of the spectrum form white light by making a color spinner. Draw around the bottom of a jar on some stiff cardboard. Cut out the circle, divide it into seven sections and paint them with the colors of the rainbow. Push a pencil through the middle and spin it on a table.
As it spins, the colored light reflecting off it merges to make white.

COLOR PRINTING

Color printing in books and magazines uses dots of magenta, yellow and cyan ink, along with black ink to make the pictures look sharper. This process is called **four-color printing**.

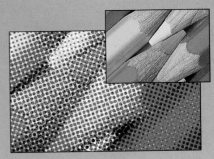

This magnified picture shows how all the colors are made up of tiny dots of magenta, yellow, cyan and black.

If you look through a magnifying glass at any picture in this book, you will see the dots which make up the image.

Colors used in four-color printing

Cyan   Magenta   Yellow   Black

Internet links

• Go to www.usborne-quicklinks.com for links to the **About Rainbows Web site** and the **Rainbow Lab Web site** to find a wealth of information about rainbows.

• Go to www.usborne-quicklinks.com for links to **The Tech Web site** and **The Franklin Institute Online Web site** to find out about light and color.

• Go to www.usborne-quicklinks.com for a link to **The Exploratorium Science Snacks Web pages** to try out lots of great light and color experiments. Find out why the sky is blue, why the sunset is red and lots more.

• Go to www.usborne-quicklinks.com for a link to the **BrainPop Web site** where you can watch a movie for a friendly introduction to lasers.

23

LIGHT BEHAVIOR

Like all electromagnetic waves, light travels incredibly quickly – about 300,000 kilometers per second when measured in a vacuum. The direction in which light waves travel is shown in diagrams by arrows. These are called **light rays**. Light waves usually travel in a straight path but may change direction when they meet an obstacle, or move from one substance into another.

The colors on the surface of soap bubbles are caused by light interference.

REFLECTION OF LIGHT

Light rays traveling toward an object are known as **incident rays**. If they hit the object and bounce off it, they are then called **reflected rays**. Each ray is reflected at the same angle as it hits the object.

When parallel light rays hit a smooth, shiny surface, they are reflected so that the reflected rays are also parallel. This is called **regular reflection**.

When parallel light rays hit a rough surface, the reflected rays are scattered in different directions. This is **diffuse reflection**. It is the most common type of reflection as most surfaces are rough (though they may not seem so unless seen with a microscope).

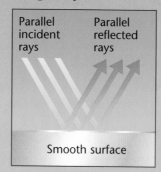

Regular reflection of light rays

Parallel incident rays

Parallel reflected rays

Smooth surface

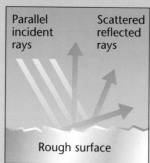

Diffuse reflection of light rays

Parallel incident rays

Scattered reflected rays

Rough surface

When you look at an object, the light that reflects off it goes directly into your eyes, so you see the object where it really is. If you look at an object in a mirror, the rays bounce off the object and then bounce off the mirror before entering your eyes. What you are looking at is the **image** of the object. In this case the image appears to be behind the mirror.

REFRACTION OF LIGHT

If light rays pass from one substance to another of a different density, their speed will change. If they are also bent, they are known as **refracted rays**. The amount of speed change and refraction depends on the change in density. Light rays speed up on moving into a less dense substance, and slow down on moving into a denser one.

For instance, light rays bouncing off objects in water can make the objects look distorted. This is because the rays are refracted as they pass out of the water into the less dense air. You can find out more about refraction on page 11.

See for yourself

To see light refraction, look at a straw in a glass of water from all sides. It seems to bend in different ways. The unbroken lines in the diagram show the real path of the light rays looking from above. But the brain assumes they travel straight, so it sees the end of the straw at X.

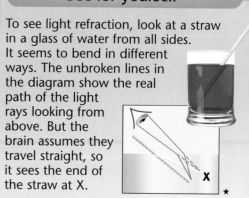

The rays of sunlight breaking through these clouds show that light travels in straight lines.

LIGHT DIFFRACTION

When light rays pass through tiny gaps, or meet the edge of an opaque object, they are diffracted, or spread out. For more about diffraction, see page 11.

LIGHT INTERFERENCE

When light rays are reflected or diffracted, their paths may cross, causing interference. See page 11 for more about interference.

As light rays interfere with each other, some wavelengths of light are strengthened and some are weakened, so certain colors become visible. The colors on a compact disc and on the surface of soap bubbles, for example, are caused by interference.

The metallic sheen on the wings of this butterfly is caused by light interference.

The shiny side of a compact disc has tiny bumps on it. When light enters the gaps between them, the waves are diffracted and interfere, so certain colors are seen at different angles.

Compact discs diffract white light, making its colors visible.

The rainbow colors on a soap bubble appear when light reflected off the outer surface of the bubble interferes with light reflected off the inner surface.

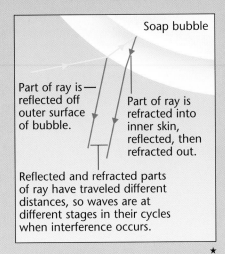

Soap bubble

Part of ray is reflected off outer surface of bubble.

Part of ray is refracted into inner skin, reflected, then refracted out.

Reflected and refracted parts of ray have traveled different distances, so waves are at different stages in their cycles when interference occurs.

The colors are constantly changing, giving a shimmering effect called **iridescence**. This is also seen on the wings of some insects and birds.

POLARIZATION

Light waves are made up of vibrations in electric and magnetic fields. The vibrations change direction many millions of times per second, but are always at right angles to the direction the wave is traveling.

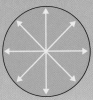

Imagine a normal light wave traveling directly into your eye. Its vibrations are in many directions, as shown here.

When light is **polarized**, the vibrations only occur in one direction, such as up and down.

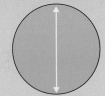

A polarized light wave is filtered so that its vibrations are in just one direction, as shown here.

Polarizing sunglasses work by filtering out all light wave vibrations that are not in a certain direction. This shields the eyes from excessive glare.

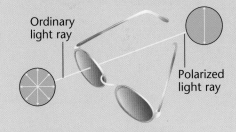

Ordinary light ray

Polarized light ray

Polarizing sunglasses only allow light vibrations through in one direction.

Internet links

• Go to www.usborne-quicklinks.com for a link to the **Sandlot Science Web site** where you can explore the intriguing world of optical illusions.

• Go to www.usborne-quicklinks.com for a link to the **Arizona State University Web site** for more about light and optics.

• Go to www.usborne-quicklinks.com for a link to the **Aquarius Web pages** where you can conduct light experiments in an underwater laboratory.

• Go to www.usborne-quicklinks.com for a link to the **PBS Diamond Web site** to discover why a diamond sparkles.

LENSES AND MIRRORS

A lens is a piece of transparent substance with curved surfaces, that makes light passing through it bend in a particular way. A **mirror** is a shiny surface that reflects nearly all of the light that hits it. Lenses and mirrors have many uses, for example in cameras and telescopes.

LENSES

Lenses are shaped so that light passing through them is bent (refracted*) in a particular way. There are two main shapes of lens: convex and concave. In a **convex lens**, one or both surfaces curve outward. In a **concave lens**, one or both surfaces curve inward.

This photograph of New York City was taken through a fish-eye lens. This curved lens creates a distorted, circular image, covering an angle of 180°.

Types of convex lenses

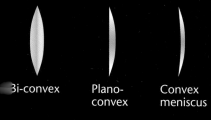

Bi-convex   Plano-   Convex
                convex   meniscus

Types of concave lenses

Bi-concave   Plano-   Concave
                concave   meniscus

Lenses are described as converging or diverging lenses, depending how the light rays are refracted. For example, a glass convex lens in air acts as a converging lens and a glass concave lens in air acts as a diverging lens.

Any point where light rays come together or appear to come from is called a **focus**. A **converging lens** causes parallel rays of light passing through it to come together at a focus.

Converging lens

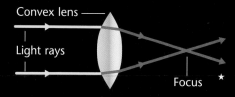

Convex lens ——

Light rays

Focus ★

A **diverging lens** makes parallel rays of light spread out.

Diverging lens

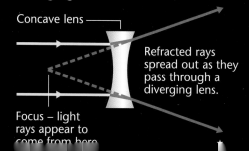

Concave lens ——

Refracted rays spread out as they pass through a diverging lens.

Focus – light rays appear to come from here

The size and position of an image seen through a converging lens depends how far the object is from the lens. If the object is very close to a converging lens, the image is upright and enlarged.

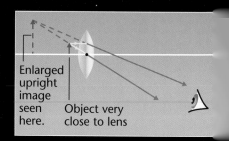

Enlarged upright image seen here.

Object very close to lens

If the object is further away from a converging lens, the image is upside down.

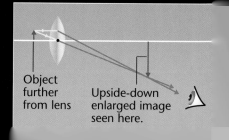

Object further from lens

Upside-down enlarged image seen here.

Your eye turns light reflected from an object into an image that can be recognized by your brain. The front part of the eye is a convex converging lens. It focuses the light rays so that they form an image on a layer called the **retina**, at the back of the eye. The image formed is upside down, but your brain then corrects this so you see things right-side up.

Human eye

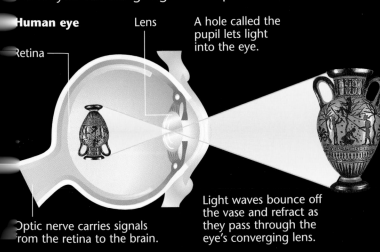

Lens

A hole called the pupil lets light into the eye.

Retina

Optic nerve carries signals from the retina to the brain.

Light waves bounce off the vase and refract as they pass through the eye's converging lens.

Distant objects are blurred for people with short sight. This is because the lenses in their eyes bend the light rays too much and the image forms in front of the retina.

Far-sighted people can't see nearby objects well. This is because the lens does not bend the light rays enough so the rays focus behind the retina.

Short sight

Rays from a distant object focus in front of the retina.

A diverging lens corrects this, focusing rays on the retina.

Diverging lens

Far sight

Rays from a near object focus beyond the retina.

A converging lens corrects this, focusing rays on the retina.

Converging lens

When light from an object hits a flat mirror straight on, it is reflected straight back. The image produced is the same size and same way up as the object but the left and right sides are switched around. The image is the same distance behind the mirror as the object is in front of the mirror.

Curved mirrors bounce light off at an angle, producing different kinds of images. A **convex mirror** curves outward. The image formed is upright and reduced in size.

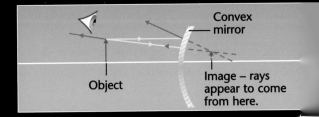

Car wing mirrors are convex.

Convex mirror

Object

Image – rays appear to come from here.

Concave mirrors curve inward. If an object is very close to the mirror, an enlarged image is produced. If the object is further away, the image is upside down. The bowl of a shiny metal spoon acts like a concave mirror.

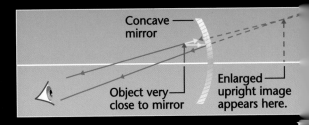

Concave mirror

Object very close to mirror

Enlarged upright image appears here.

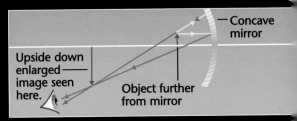

Concave mirror

Upside down enlarged image seen here.

Object further from mirror

See for yourself

Look at your reflection in the bowl of a shiny metal spoon. If you hold the spoon very close to your face, the reflection will be enlarged. If you hold it a little further away, the reflection will be upside down. Look at the two diagrams at the bottom of the column on the right to see why this happens.

Internet links

• Go to **www.usborne-quicklinks.com** for a link to the **Beakman & Jax Web pages** to discover how glasses work by bending light.

• Go to **www.usborne-quicklinks.com** for a link to the **Exploratorium Science Snacks Web site** to find experiments which help to explain reflection and refraction.

• Go to **www.usborne-quicklinks.com** for a link to the **ExploreScience Web site** for interactive optic activities.

OPTICAL INSTRUMENTS

Optical instruments use combinations of lenses and mirrors to produce a particular type of image, for example, an image that appears larger than when viewed with the eye alone. These pages show some of the many kinds of optical instruments.

Binoculars use lenses to magnify objects.

OPTICAL MICROSCOPES

Optical microscopes use lenses to make small objects look bigger. Simple ones, such as a magnifying glass, have only one lens. More complex ones use two lenses or more.

Inside a **compound optical microscope**, the object is first magnified by the **objective lens**. It is further magnified by the **eyepiece**, which produces the final image. Some optical microscopes can magnify up to 2,000 times.

A compound optical microscope

1. **Eyepiece**. This refracts (bends) light from the objective lens, turns the image right-side up, and makes it look much bigger.

2. **Focusing knob**. This controls the sharpness and clarity of the image.

3. **Body tube**

4. **Nosepiece**. This holds three objective lenses, each giving a different magnification. It is swiveled around to change between them.

5. **Objective lens**. This refracts light from the object to form a larger, upside-down image. The eyepiece then further magnifies this image.

6. **Stage**. The object to be magnified goes on here.

7. **Object**

8. **Mirror**. This reflects daylight or lamplight through a hole in the stage onto the object.

Using magnifying lenses, scientists can learn about the structure of tiny living things, such as this ladybug.

On its own, the eye can only see small objects separately if they are at least a quarter of a millimeter apart. A microscope can show you objects separately that are up to 1,000 times closer together than this.

The tiny hairs on the ladybug's mouthparts are too small to be seen with the eye alone, but are easy to make out under a microscope's magnifying lens.

PERISCOPES

A **periscope** is an upright tube with prisms at each end. Prisms are glass shapes with two flat surfaces at an angle to each other. In a periscope they are used to reflect light around corners, which allows you to see something when you are far below it. For instance, periscopes are used in submarines to look above the surface of the water.

Diagram of a periscope

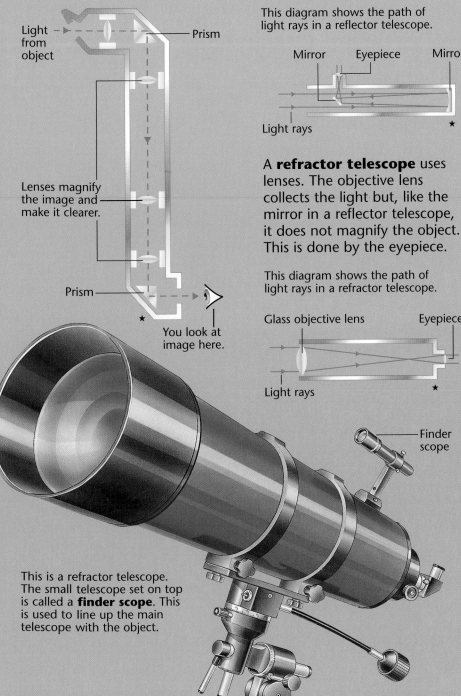

Light from object

Prism

Lenses magnify the image and make it clearer.

Prism

You look at image here.

This is a refractor telescope. The small telescope set on top is called a **finder scope**. This is used to line up the main telescope with the object.

Finder scope

TELESCOPES

Telescopes are used to make distant objects appear closer and therefore larger. They are often used for looking at the stars. There are two main types: reflector and refractor telescopes.

A **reflector telescope** uses a curved mirror to collect light. The light then reflects off a second mirror and an image is focused in front of the eyepiece, which magnifies it.

This diagram shows the path of light rays in a reflector telescope.

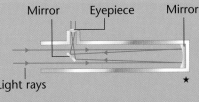

Mirror   Eyepiece   Mirror

Light rays

A **refractor telescope** uses lenses. The objective lens collects the light but, like the mirror in a reflector telescope, it does not magnify the object. This is done by the eyepiece.

This diagram shows the path of light rays in a refractor telescope.

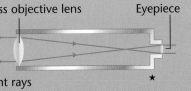

Glass objective lens   Eyepiece

Light rays

CAMERAS

Cameras are optical instruments that record pictures. They use lenses to focus light onto film or some other device that saves the picture so that you can look at it again later. Early cameras stored pictures on sheets of glass or metal coated with light-sensitive substances. Today, most cameras use light-sensitive film. Digital cameras, invented in the 1990s, store pictures electronically.

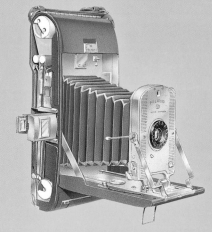

This is an early Polaroid camera. Polaroid film develops rapidly, so you see the picture just after you take it.

CAMERA PRINCIPLES

Light enters a camera through a lens. The amount of light that is let in is called the **exposure**. Exposure is controlled by two things. First, an adjustable hole called an **aperture** determines how much light gets into the camera. Second, a flap called a **shutter** controls how long light is allowed to fall on the film.

Single-lens reflex (SLR) camera

In this type of camera, light entering the lens is reflected off a mirror and refracted through a prism to a little window called the **viewfinder**. This lets the photographer see exactly what the lens sees.

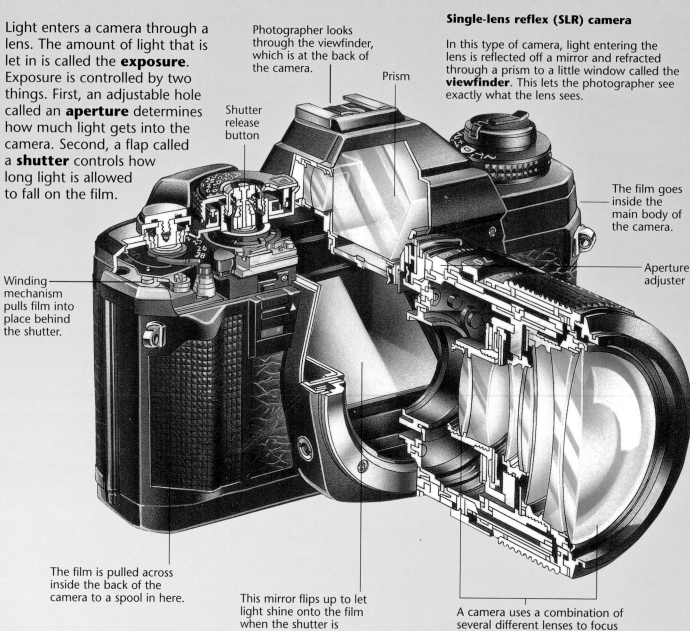

Photographer looks through the viewfinder, which is at the back of the camera.

Prism

Shutter release button

The film goes inside the main body of the camera.

Aperture adjuster

Winding mechanism pulls film into place behind the shutter.

The film is pulled across inside the back of the camera to a spool in here.

This mirror flips up to let light shine onto the film when the shutter is released.

A camera uses a combination of several different lenses to focus light from an object onto the film.

PHOTOGRAPHIC FILM

Photographic film is coated with silver nitrate, a light-sensitive chemical. How the film reacts depends on the amount of light that reaches it.

The exposed film is dipped into chemicals to produce the images and stop the film from being sensitive to any more light. This process is called **developing**.

Positive film (also called **transparency** or **slide film**). This shows images with the correct colors.

Negative film. The light parts of the piano keyboard in the picture appear dark and the dark parts appear light.

Developed negative film is projected onto light-sensitive paper to make the final print.

MOVING PICTURES

Motion-picture cameras record images on very long strips of photographic film. They take 25 separate pictures, called **frames**, every second. The film is developed in the same way as film from a normal camera.

The film is held in a cassette which clips onto the camera.

To watch the film, it is wound through a projector at a rate of 25 frames per second. The frames move so fast that you see the next frame before the last one fades in your brain. This is called **persistent vision**.

x

* Binary code, 44.

See for yourself

You can demonstrate persistent vision by making your own "movie" flip book.

On the back page of a small pad of paper draw a simple character. Turn over the page and trace this image, making slight changes to show the character moving. Draw at least 20 more images, changing each one a little.

When you flip the pad, the images appear as one moving picture.

TELEVISION CAMERAS

Television cameras do not use film, but turn the light that enters them into a series of electrical signals. These signals are sent down a cable and are either transmitted as a live broadcast, or recorded onto tape or computer to be transmitted at another time.

A television studio camera is heavy and is supported by a stand.

CAMCORDERS

A **video camcorder** is a combined TV camera and video recorder. Lenses direct an image onto a tiny light-sensitive electronic part called a **charge-coupled device (CCD)**. The CCD produces electrical signals which are recorded onto videotape.

This small camcorder can fit in the palm of your hand.

DIGITAL CAMERAS

Digital cameras record images onto a CCD. The images are broken down into tiny colored squares called **pixels**. Information about the pixels is stored in the camera's memory as binary code*. To print the picture or see it on a computer screen, the pixels recombine, forming a complete picture.

The degree of detail in a picture is called its **resolution**. The more pixels that a digital camera creates in an image, the higher the image's resolution.

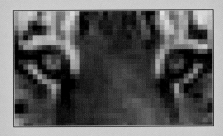

Low-resolution image

High-resolution image

Internet links

• Go to **www.usborne-quicklinks.com** for a link to **The Franklin Institute Online Web site** to learn about the early history of cameras and photography.

• Go to **www.usborne-quicklinks.com** for a link to the **UK's National Museum of Photography, Film & Television Web site** for lots of information.

• Go to **www.usborne-quicklinks.com** for a link to the **BrainPop Web site** to watch a fun movie on photography.

• Go to **www.usborne-quicklinks.com** for links to the **Pentax Web site**, the **Canon Web site**, the **Nikon Web site** and the **Minolta Web site** where you can find out about the latest photographical equipment available from some of the most famous manufacturers.

31

TV AND RADIO

The first radio transmissions were made about 100 years ago. Television was invented in 1926. The first signals could only be sent over very short distances, but today satellites can instantly broadcast clear signals around the world.

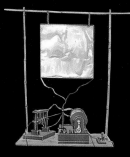

This early radio was invented by Marconi. It was called a marconiphone.

BROADCASTING

Most radio and television shows are broadcast as **radio waves**. These are a band of waves in the electromagnetic spectrum* with a range of different frequencies* and wavelengths*.

Radio waves

Radio waves are the longest waves in the electromagnetic spectrum.

Before broadcasting, sounds and images first have to be converted into electrical signals. Sounds are made into electrical signals by microphones. Cameras create electrical signals from images.

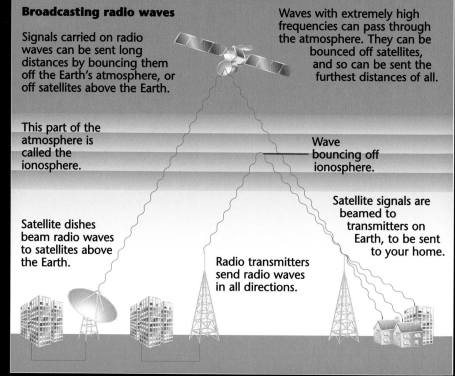

Broadcasting radio waves

Signals carried on radio waves can be sent long distances by bouncing them off the Earth's atmosphere, or off satellites above the Earth.

Waves with extremely high frequencies can pass through the atmosphere. They can be bounced off satellites, and so can be sent the furthest distances of all.

This part of the atmosphere is called the ionosphere.

Wave bouncing off ionosphere.

Satellite dishes beam radio waves to satellites above the Earth.

Radio transmitters send radio waves in all directions.

Satellite signals are beamed to transmitters on Earth, to be sent to your home.

MODULATION

To enable them to be broadcast, electrical signals have to be altered, using a method called **modulation**. This is done by mixing the electrical sound and picture signals with radio waves, called **carrier waves**.

As a result of modulation, the shape of the carrier wave varies depending on the electrical sound and picture signals. The picture on the right shows an example of this.

With **frequency modulation (FM)** the electrical signals are altered to match the frequency of the carrier wave. With **amplitude modulation (AM)** the electrical signals are altered to match the amplitude* (strength) of the carrier wave.

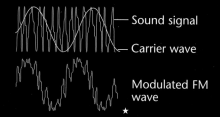

Sound signal

Carrier wave

Modulated FM wave

HOW A RADIO WORKS

A radio works by receiving modulated radio waves through its antenna, and then converting them back into very weak electrical signals.

Radio receives many different signals. Tuner is adjusted to select wavelength of broadcast required.

The signal is strengthened (amplified) and a loudspeaker turns it into a sound that can be heard.

* Amplitude, 9; Electromagnetic spectrum, 18-19; Frequency, Wavelength, 9.

Television signals are carried by radio waves. As well as the sound signals, the waves carry picture signals. A television converts these signals into sound and pictures. The sound is converted in the same way as in a radio. The picture signals are converted into pictures by a **cathode ray tube**. The pictures are built up from about 350,000 tiny shapes called **pixels** (short for picture elements).

A cathode ray tube

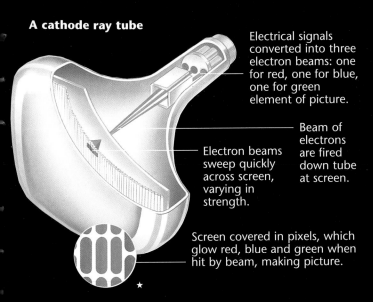

Electrical signals converted into three electron beams: one for red, one for blue, one for green element of picture.

Beam of electrons are fired down tube at screen.

Electron beams sweep quickly across screen, varying in strength.

Screen covered in pixels, which glow red, blue and green when hit by beam, making picture.

CABLE BROADCASTING

TV and radio signals can be carried along cables, too. The cables can convey more signals than when they are transmitted through the air, so more channels are available. A vast network of underground cables exists. These can also be used to carry phone signals.

Fiber-optic cables are used for carrying television and radio signals.

DIGITAL BROADCASTING

By 2010 most radio and television broadcasting will be done **digitally**. Digital signals are electrical signals which carry information as a code made up of millions and millions of just two components: either "on" (1) or "off" (0).

The digital code is mixed onto – and then carried by – radio waves. Digital information can be compressed (see *Transmission Speed*, page 51, for an example) so far more can be sent. As a result, broadcasters can offer more channels than previously.

Digital broadcasting makes it possible to communicate in two directions. As a result, you can send information back through your TV, to order programs to watch whenever you want, or to buy things, or even to take part in games and competitions. This is called **interactive TV**.

This TV shows an interactive game to play during a soccer game.

Competitors predict the scorers of goals and the game's outcome. Their predictions are registered with the TV company and if they are right they win instant prizes.

SATELLITE TV

Satellite TV companies bounce signals off space satellites, to be received directly by a small dish that is fixed to the side of your home.

The dish focuses the TV signal onto a receiver. The signals travel along a cable to a television set.

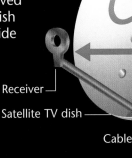

Receiver

Satellite TV dish

Cable

See for yourself

Put a magnifying glass up close to your TV set while it is on. Look carefully and you'll be able to see the pixels that make up the picture.

Internet links

• Go to **www.usborne-quicklinks.com** for a link to the **Surfing the Aether Web site** to explore the history of radio technology by following a time line.

• Go to **www.usborne-quicklinks.com** for links to the **PBS People and Discoveries Web site** where you can read about Marconi's invention, try a radio transmission activity and learn more about radio. You can also learn more about the history of television.

• Go to **www.usborne-quicklinks.com** for a link to the **BrainPop Web site** where you can watch a movie and then test your knowledge by trying to answer a quiz about radio.

ELECTRICITY

Lightning is a form of electricity.

Electricity is a useful form of energy. It can easily be converted to other forms of energy, such as heat or light, and it can flow along cables, which makes it easy to transport. Electricity is used to power many devices, from kettles to computers, and to provide heat and light in homes, offices and factories.

ELECTRIC CHARGE

All matter is made up of tiny units called **atoms**. In the middle of each atom is a **nucleus**. This contains particles called **protons** which have a positive charge and **neutrons** which have no charge. Negatively charged particles called **electrons** whizz around the nucleus. Normally, the number of protons and electrons is equal. Their charges cancel each other out so the atom is electrically neutral.

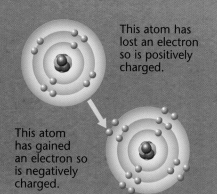

Proton (positive charge)

Neutron (no charge)

Electron (negative charge)

An atom can gain or lose electrons. If it gains electrons, it becomes negatively charged (–). If it loses electrons, it becomes positively charged (+).

This atom has lost an electron so is positively charged.

This atom has gained an electron so is negatively charged.

If charged particles are close enough to each other, they have an effect on each other known as an **electric force**. The area in which this force has an effect is called an **electric field**.

Particles with opposite charges (positive and negative charges) attract each other. Particles with the same type of charge, for example two positively charged particles, push each other away.

Atoms with opposite charges attract each other.

Atoms with the same charge push each other away.

Electricity is the effect caused by the presence or movement of charged particles.

ELECTRIC CURRENT

In certain substances, such as metals, some electrons are not held tightly by the atoms and can move between them. If they are made to move, there is a flow of electric charge called an **electric current**. Substances through which current can flow are called **conductors**. Those substances, such as plastic, which cannot conduct current, are called **insulators**.

Wood and plastic are insulators.

Aluminum foil is a conductor.

Insulated wires are electrical wires, usually made of copper, covered with plastic to insulate them.

Electrons cannot flow.

Electrons can flow and make a current.

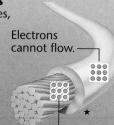

See for yourself

To see how charges affect each other, tape two equal lengths of nylon thread to the top of a door frame, spaced about 1in apart. Tie a balloon to each thread, so that they touch and hang at the same height. Rub the balloons with a wool scarf or sweater. The balloons become negatively charged and move away from each other. If you put your hand in between the balloons, they move toward your hand, which has a positive charge.

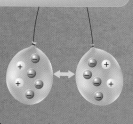

Matching charges repel each other.

STATIC ELECTRICITY

Some insulating materials become charged when rubbed. This happens because electrons from one material are transferred to the other. The charge cannot flow away because there is no conductor, so it builds up on the surface of the material. Electrical charge that is held by a material is called **static electricity**.

The diagrams below show how static electricity builds up if you rub a balloon on a wool sweater.

Before they are rubbed, the balloon and the sweater are electrically neutral.

As they are rubbed, some electrons from the sweater move to the balloon. This becomes negatively charged, and the sweater becomes positively charged. They cling together because their opposite charges attract each other.

Equipment such as laser printers and photocopiers use static electricity as part of their printing process.

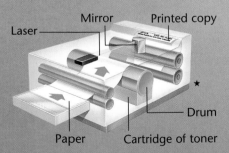

Laser — Mirror — Printed copy

Paper — Cartridge of toner — Drum

In a laser printer, a laser beam reflected by a mirror makes dots of static electricity on a drum. Toner clings to the dots of static and is pressed onto the paper.

LIGHTNING

Lightning is caused by static electricity that builds up when falling water droplets and rising ice crystals rub against each other in storm clouds.

Water droplets and ice crystals become charged as they rub against each other and the air.

Positive charges gather at the top of the cloud and negative charges in the base. As this happens, positive charges collect together on the ground beneath the cloud.

A giant spark, called a **leader stroke**, flashes out from the cloud, seeking a point with the opposite charge on the ground. When it finds it, it makes a path which is followed by a powerful stroke of lightning from the ground to the cloud. This is called the **return stroke**.

Lightning contains a vast amount of electrical energy, which is changed into light, heat and sound (thunder).

A build-up of negative charge at the base of a storm cloud causes a build-up of positive charge in the ground below.

When lightning strikes, an electric current flows between the cloud and the ground, leaving them both electrically neutral.

The air heated by the flashes of lightning expands very rapidly. This makes the noise that we hear as **thunder**. Light travels faster than sound, so unless the storm cloud is directly overhead, you see the lightning before you hear the thunder.

A stroke of lightning branches out in many directions as it seeks its way to the ground.

Internet links

• Go to **www.usborne-quicklinks.com** to watch a movie on the **BrainPop Web site**.

• Go to **www.usborne-quicklinks.com** for a link to the **Edison International Web site** to meet the energy heroes.

• Go to **www.usborne-quicklinks.com** for a link to the **Boston Museum of Science Web site** for more fun facts.

• Go to **www.usborne-quicklinks.com** for a link to the **Yorkshire Electricity Web site** for interactive electricity activities.

• Go to **www.usborne-quicklinks.com** for a link to the **Electron Discovery Web pages** to read about the electron's discovery.

• Go to **www.usborne-quicklinks.com** for a link to the **Miami Museum of Science Web site** for fun experiments.

• Go to **www.usborne-quicklinks.com** for a link to the **National Geographic Web site** to learn all about lightning.

CIRCUITS

An electric current flows from one place to another as a result of something called **potential difference**. This is similar to the pressure difference that causes water to flow through pipes. Potential difference is measured in **volts (V)** and is also called **voltage**. Current is measured in units called **amperes (amps)**.

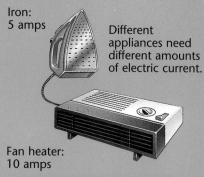

Iron:
5 amps

Different appliances need different amounts of electric current.

Fan heater:
10 amps

For an electric current to keep flowing there must be a power source, such as a battery (see opposite page), joined to an unbroken conducting pathway, such as a loop of copper wire. This pathway is called an **electric circuit**. The power source has two ends with opposite charges, called **poles** or **terminals**. These are where the circuit starts and finishes.

Terminals

A potential difference exists between the terminals of a battery. When they are joined, a circuit is formed and a current flows.

Components, such as bulbs, can be added to a circuit. These convert the electrical energy carried by the current into other forms of energy such as light and heat. The components in a circuit can be arranged in two ways: in series or in parallel.

In a **series circuit**, the current passes through the components one after the other. If one component is not working, it breaks the circuit and no current flows. For example, in a chain of Christmas lights, if one bulb fails, the current to the others is cut off.

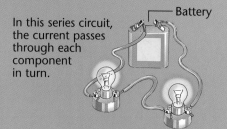

In this series circuit, the current passes through each component in turn.

— Battery

A **parallel circuit** has more than one path for the current. If a component in one path does not work, current continues to flow through the other path.

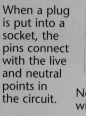

In this parallel circuit, the current passes through the components by different paths at the same time.

ELECTRICITY AT HOME

Household electricity is 240V in some countries and 110V in others. These large voltages can give you a deadly electric shock. Appliances are protected by **fuses** containing very thin pieces of wire. These melt, and cut off the current if it is too large.

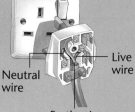

Fuse with part of cover removed

Fuse wire

Electricity is carried to different parts of a house by parallel circuits. These circuits contain two wires called the **live** and **neutral wires**, which carry the current. In some countries there is also an **earth wire**. This is a safety device. It provides a path to the ground through which electric current can escape if the plug develops a fault.

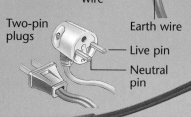

When a plug is put into a socket, the pins connect with the live and neutral points in the circuit.

Live wire

Neutral wire

Earth wire

Two-pin plugs

Live pin

Neutral pin

This electricity substation reduces to a lower level the massive voltage it receives from the main power station. The current travels along cables to homes and factories.

BATTERIES

A **battery** is a store of chemical energy that can be converted to electrical energy. The most common type of battery used at home is called a **dry cell**. It contains a paste called an **electrolyte** which contains charged particles that can move. Chemical reactions make the charges separate. Positive charges move to one terminal and negative ones move to the other.

Batteries produce an electric current that moves in a single direction. This is called **direct current** (**DC**).

Cutaway view of a dry cell

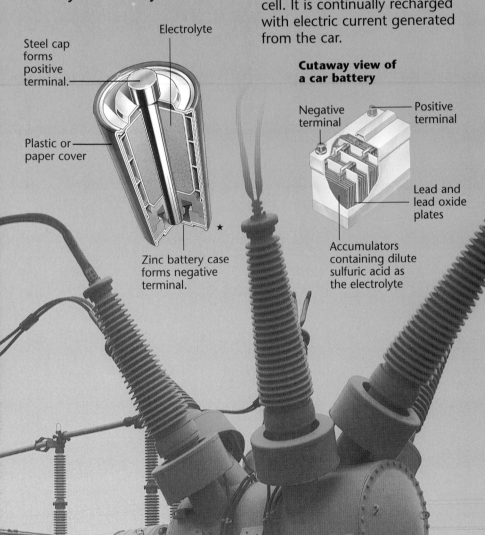

Steel cap forms positive terminal.

Electrolyte

Plastic or paper cover

Zinc battery case forms negative terminal.

A 1.5V battery, such as the type used in a personal stereo, is called a **single cell**. Larger batteries are made up of several single cells.

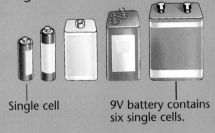

Single cell

9V battery contains six single cells.

Dry cells are **primary cells**. When the chemicals in the electrolyte run out, the battery is finished. **Secondary cells**, or **accumulators**, are batteries that can be recharged. A car battery is a type of secondary cell. It is continually recharged with electric current generated from the car.

Cutaway view of a car battery

Negative terminal

Positive terminal

Lead and lead oxide plates

Accumulators containing dilute sulfuric acid as the electrolyte

A **solar cell** converts the Sun's energy into electricity. Sunlight falling on the layers of silicon makes the electrons move, creating a potential difference between the two layers.

Solar cells like this one are used in pocket calculators.

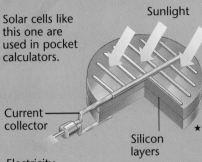

Sunlight

Current collector

Silicon layers

Electricity

See for yourself

To make a simple battery, draw around a coin to make twelve circles each on a sheet of foil and a paper towel, then cut them out. Dampen the paper circles in a cup of water with ten teaspoons of salt stirred in.

You need 12 copper coins. Pile the circles in groups of three (a cell), made up of one foil, one paper and one coin. Tape the bare end of a piece of insulated copper wire to the bottom of the pile, and another wire to the top. Touch the other two ends together. In a dark room you should see a spark.

Internet links

• Go to **www.usborne-quicklinks.com** for a link to the **Cornwallis Net Web site** where you can find an easy-to-read introduction to electricity and circuits.

• Go to **www.usborne-quicklinks.com** for a link to the **Exploratorium Science Snacks Web pages** to discover how to do safe and simple electricity experiments.

MAGNETISM

Magnetism is an invisible force that attracts some metals, especially iron and steel. Materials that create this force are said to be **magnetic** and are called **magnets**.

POLES

If you float a magnet in water or hang it from a thread tied around its middle, it will always point in a north-south direction. The part of the magnet that points north is the **north** or **north-seeking pole**. The other is the **south** or **south-seeking pole**.

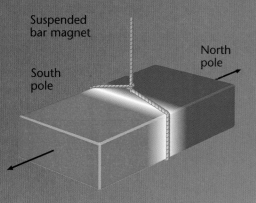

Suspended
bar magnet

South
pole

North
pole

A north and a south pole of two magnets will pull toward or **attract** each other. Two north or two south poles will push each other away. This is called **repulsion**.

Like poles repel each other.

Unlike poles attract each other.

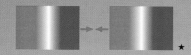

TYPES OF MAGNETS

Materials that can easily be magnetized (turned into magnets) are said to be **ferromagnetic**. They can be described as hard or soft.

Soft ferromagnetic materials such as iron quickly lose their magnetic properties. Magnets made from these materials are called **temporary magnets**. Hard ferromagnetic materials such as steel keep their magnetic properties for much longer. They are used to make **permanent magnets**.

Each paper clip in this chain has become magnetized by contact with the magnet. Each is a temporary magnet.

If the magnet is removed, the clips will lose their magnetism.

A compass needle is a permanent magnet. It points to the Earth's magnetic north pole.

Migrating terns like these may use the Earth's magnetic field to guide them.

DIPOLES AND DOMAINS

A ferromagnetic material has molecules which behave like tiny magnets. They are known as **dipoles** and are grouped in **domains**, in which they all point the same way. When the material is magnetized, all the domains become ordered and point the same way. The material loses its magnetism if its domains become jumbled up again.

When magnetic material is in a non-magnetized state, the domains are jumbled up.

When it is magnetized, the domains line up, with their poles all pointing the same way.

Ordered dipoles collectively form a magnet, but individually, each one is trying to flip round, as its poles are attracted to the opposite poles of the whole magnet. As they turn, the magnet loses its magnetism.

A metal **keeper** across a magnet's ends helps it to stay magnetic. The keeper becomes magnetized and attracts the magnet's dipoles to its poles.

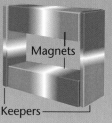

Magnets

Keepers

MAGNETIC FIELDS

The region around a magnet in which objects are affected by its magnetic force is called a **magnetic field**. The strength and direction of the magnetic field are shown by **magnetic flux lines**. The arrows on the lines show the direction. The magnetic field is strongest where the lines are close together.

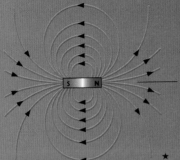

Magnetic flux lines showing the direction of the magnetic field around a bar magnet

The lines are closest near the poles, where the field is strongest.

The Earth itself has a magnetic field. It acts as though it has a giant bar magnet through its middle. The north pole of a compass points towards a point called **magnetic north**, its south pole points to **magnetic south**. These are different from the geographical North and South Poles.

These magnetic flux lines show the direction of the magnetic field around the Earth.

ELECTROMAGNETISM

When an electric current flows through a wire, it produces a magnetic field around it. This effect is called **electromagnetism**.

The magnetic field of the wire can be made stronger if the wire is wound in a coil. When a current is passed through the coil, the coil behaves like a bar magnet and is called a **solenoid**. The region inside the coil is called the **core**.

If a solenoid has a rod of a soft ferromagnetic material such as iron placed inside it, the rod is quickly magnetized and adds its own magnetic field to that of the solenoid. Together the solenoid and the ferromagnetic core make an **electromagnet**. You can find out more about the uses of electromagnets over the page.

A simple electromagnet

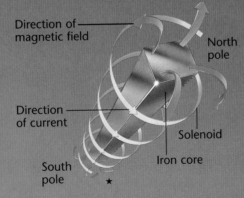

Direction of magnetic field

North pole

Direction of current

Solenoid

Iron core

South pole

The position of the north and south poles in an electromagnet depends on the direction of the current flowing through the wire.

Viewed end-on, current flowing counterclockwise gives a north pole.

Current flowing clockwise gives a south pole.

See for yourself

To see magnetic flux lines, sprinkle some iron filings onto a sheet of clear plastic or a piece of white paper, then hold a magnet underneath. The iron filings will move to show the pattern of the magnetic field.

Clear plastic sheet

Internet links

• Go to **www.usborne-quicklinks.com** for a link to the **BrainPop Web site** to see a movie and answer a quiz about magnets.

• Go to **www.usborne-quicklinks.com** for a link to the **Explore Science Web site** for interactive magentism activities.

• Go to **www.usborne-quicklinks.com** for a link to the **Exploratorium Science Snacks Web pages** to try out some magnetism experiments.

• Go to **www.usborne-quicklinks.com** for a link to the **Magnetic Fields Web pages** to read all about magnetic fields.

• Go to **www.usborne-quicklinks.com** for a link to the **Magnets and GMR Materials Web pages** to see interactive models of magnetic materials.

USING ELECTROMAGNETS

Electromagnets often contain iron, a soft ferromagnetic material. The iron loses almost all of its magnetism when the current through the electromagnet is switched off. For this reason, electromagnets have many uses, such as in switches, bells and buzzers.

When you press the button of an electric bell, for example, current flows through the coils of an electromagnet and attracts a metal arm. As the arm moves closer to the electromagnet, it loses touch with the contact through which the current is flowing, breaking the circuit. The arm is pulled back by a spring, making a hammer hit a bell. This completes the circuit and the cycle begins again.

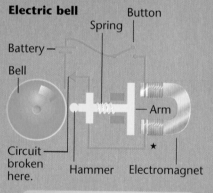

Electric bell

Button
Spring
Battery—
Bell
Arm
Circuit broken here.
Hammer   Electromagnet

See for yourself

You can make an electromagnet using a 4.5V battery, a pencil, a large iron nail and some insulated copper wire. To make a solenoid*, wind the wire tightly around the pencil, and tape both ends to the battery. Your electromagnet should be strong enough to affect a compass needle, but too weak to pick anything up. If you replace the pencil with the nail, you will have an electromagnet that can pick up paper clips.

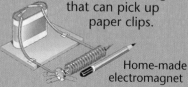

Home-made electromagnet

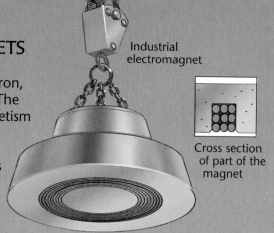

Industrial electromagnet

Cross section of part of the magnet

Very powerful electromagnets are used in steelworks to lift heavy loads. When current flows through the coil of wire, the iron becomes magnetized. It attracts steel, which can be moved from one place to another. When the current is switched off, the electromagnet releases its load.

Magnetic levitation (maglev) trains have electromagnets on the bottom. They run on tracks with electromagnets on them. The magnets repel each other, so the train hovers just above the track. This reduces the amount of friction between the train and the track, so the train needs less energy to make it move.

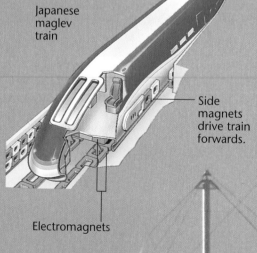

Japanese maglev train

Side magnets drive train forwards.

Electromagnets

ELECTRIC MOTORS

Electric motors change electrical energy into movement. A simple electric motor (see picture below) contains a flat coil of wire called an **armature** between two magnets.

When current flows through the armature, the combination of the electromagnetic field of the armature and the magnetic fields of the magnets pushes one side of the armature up and the other side down.

A simple electric motor

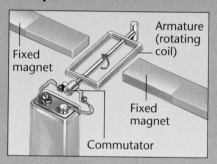

Armature (rotating coil)
Fixed magnet
Fixed magnet
Commutator

When the armature is in an upright position, a device called a **commutator** causes the direction of the electric current to be reversed, so the magnetic field of the armature is reversed. The side of the armature that was pushed up is now pulled down. The armature completes its circle and the cycle begins again.

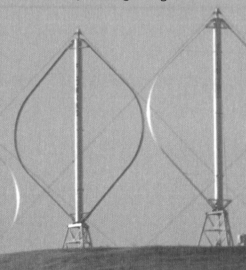

USES FOR MOTORS

Electric motors are used in all kinds of equipment, from washing machines and hairdryers to battery-driven toy cars and model trains. Tiny **micromotors** (see picture below) are being developed for use in microsurgery and space research.

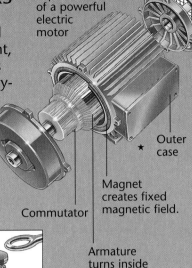

Exploded view of a powerful electric motor

★ Outer case

Commutator

Magnet creates fixed magnetic field.

Armature turns inside field.

This Toshiba micromotor is 0.8mm wide – about the same as the eye of the needle next to it.

GENERATING ELECTRICITY

A **dynamo** or **generator** is a machine for converting movement energy into electrical energy. It works rather like an electric motor in reverse. The diagrams below show how a generator produces electricity. As the armature turns between the two magnets, an electric current starts to flow. As the armature passes through its upright position, the direction of the current changes. This type of current is called **alternating current** (**AC**).

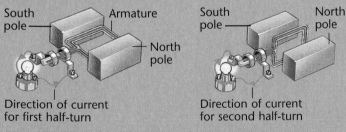

South pole

Armature

North pole

Direction of current for first half-turn

South pole

North pole

Direction of current for second half-turn

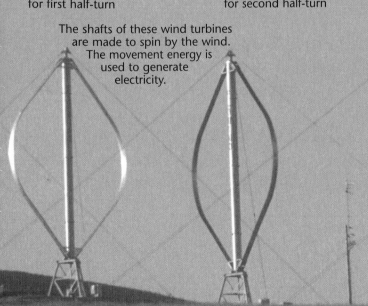

The shafts of these wind turbines are made to spin by the wind. The movement energy is used to generate electricity.

A **bicycle dynamo** is a type of generator. It uses the movement energy from a wheel to produce electric current to light a lamp.

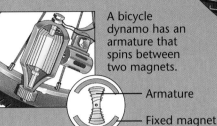

A bicycle dynamo has an armature that spins between two magnets.

Armature

Fixed magnet

Electricity is generated on a larger scale in **power stations**. Many power stations use heat energy from burning coal to boil water and turn it to steam. The pressure of the steam is used to spin the shaft of a machine called a **turbine**. This then turns the shaft of a huge generator and produces alternating current.

Generator containing coils

Steam from water heated by furnaces

Cutaway of steam turbine

Turbines turned by force of steam

Electricity is produced.

★

Steam escapes here.

Generators can be powered by many different kinds of energy. Wind turbines, for example, use the energy of moving air (wind) to generate electricity.

Internet links

• Go to **www.usborne-quicklinks.com** for a link to the **How Stuff Works Web site** to find out more about what electric motors are used for and how they work.

• Go to **www.usborne-quicklinks.com** for a link to the **Beakman's Electric Motor Web pages** where you can follow clear instructions and simple diagrams to discover how a simple electric motor is built.

• Go to **www.usborne-quicklinks.com** for links to the **Florida State University Web site** to see amazing animations to find out how metal detectors use magnetism. You can also find out how an electrical generator works.

• Go to **www.usborne-quicklinks.com** for links to the **ABC News Web site** and the **NASA New Science Web pages** where you can read articles and explore interactive models of trains and space craft powered by magnetic levitation.

ELECTRONICS

Electronics is the use of devices called **electronic components** to control the way electric current flows around a circuit, making it do particular tasks. A circuit controlled in this way is called an **electronic circuit**. All sorts of machines, such as TVs, robots and computers, use electronic circuits.

Copper tracks on the back of this Veroboard link electronic components to form a circuit.

BUILDING CIRCUITS

Electronic circuits can be made up using different components. The simple circuit below, for instance, contains a resistor (see right).

Battery · Resistor · Bulb

Circuits can be mapped out using diagrams like the one below. Each component is shown using a different circuit symbol. The main circuit symbols can be found together on page 54.

Circuit diagram of circuit above

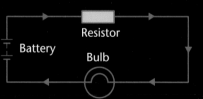

Battery · Resistor · Bulb

You can make simple circuits using **Veroboard**. This has rows of holes and copper tracks on the back. Components are pushed through from the front, then their legs are soldered onto the tracks to form a circuit. **Printed circuit boards (PCBs)** are plastic boards which are imprinted with metal tracks. They are used, for example, in televisions. **Integrated circuits** are tiny circuits engraved onto small slices of silicon.

RESISTANCE

The ability of a substance to restrict the flow of electric current is known as **resistance**. All the parts in an electric circuit have a certain amount of resistance, and this reduces the amount of current that is able to flow around it in a certain time. When a substance resists an electric current, it converts some of the electrical energy into heat or light.

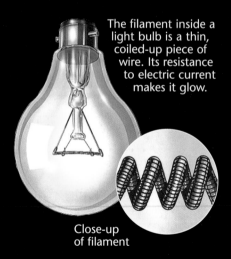

The filament inside a light bulb is a thin, coiled-up piece of wire. Its resistance to electric current makes it glow.

Close-up of filament

Resistance is measured in units called **ohms**, named after Georg Ohm, a nineteenth-century physicist.

Ω

The Greek letter omega is used as a symbol for ohms.

Resistors are electronic components which reduce the flow of current. Resistors have three or four color-coded stripes on them which show how much resistance they give.

Resistor color code chart	
1st to 3rd stripes	**4th stripe**
0 1 2 3 4 5 6 7 8 9	Gold ±5% Silver ±10% No fourth stripe ±20%

The first two stripes on a resistor stand for numbers. The third tells how many zeros to put on the end. The fourth stripe tells you the rating's range. The stripes on the resistor below, for example, are blue (6), red (2), black (0) and gold (±5%), so it has a resistance of 62 ohms, plus or minus 5%.

The stripes on this resistor show that it gives between 58.9 and 65.1Ω of resistance.

See for yourself

Using the color code chart above, try to determine which of these two resistors has the highest ohm rating. (Answer on page 63.)

TYPES OF COMPONENTS

There are several types of electronic components. Each one is designed to do a different job in an electronic circuit. For example, different kinds of resistors are designed to resist current by greater or lesser amounts in different conditions.

A **variable resistor**, or **rheostat**, can be adjusted to give different amounts of resistance. The volume control on a radio uses a variable resistor to change the amount of current. This varies the amount of electrical energy that is converted to sound energy.

Variable resistor

A **thermistor** is a heat-sensitive resistor. Its resistance falls as the temperature rises, and rises as the temperature falls. They are used in some fire alarms to sense when a room is too hot.

Thermistor

Diodes allow the current to flow through them in only one direction. A **light-emitting diode (LED)** glows when current flows through it.

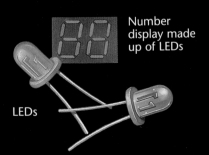

Number display made up of LEDs

LEDs

On this printed circuit board, the black oblong shapes contain integrated circuits. They are connected to each other and to other components by metal tracks.

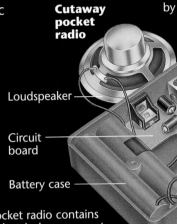

Cutaway pocket radio

Antenna. This picks up signals which are then amplified (strengthened) by transistors.

Integrated circuit contains tiny transistors.

Loudspeaker

Circuit board

Battery case

Tuning control

Volume control (containing variable resistor)

Capacitors

This pocket radio contains many electrical components arranged in a circuit called an **amplifier circuit**.

Transistors are electronic switches. A transistor has three legs, called the **base**, the **collector** and the **emitter**. When a small current flows into the base leg, the transistor allows a larger current to flow between the collector and the emitter. The transistor is then switched on. When no current flows to the base leg the transistor is off.

Transistor

This diagram shows the currents (white arrows) that flow through a transistor in a circuit.

Base — From power source

Emitter

Collector

To power source

From power source

Capacitors store up electrical energy and release it when it is needed. A television uses capacitors to build up and store very high voltages.

Capacitors

There are different kinds of capacitors.

Internet links

• Go to **www.usborne-quicklinks.com** for a link to the **Basic Electronics Web site** for an introduction to electronics.

• Go to **www.usborne-quicklinks.com** for a link to **The Xtal Set Society Web site** to discover how to build a crystal radio.

• Go to **www.usborne-quicklinks.com** for a link to the **Electrical and Electronic Symbols Web pages** where you can test your knowledge of circuit symbols.

• Go to **www.usborne-quicklinks.com** for links to the **Florida State University Web pages** where you can try interactive electronics activities about resistance and resistor color codes.

• Go to **www.usborne-quicklinks.com** for a link to the **University of Maryland Web site** for a brief history of electronics.

DIGITAL ELECTRONICS

Digital electronics is a form of electronics that uses pulses of electricity instead of continuously flowing, or **analog**, electricity. All sorts of electronic equipment, from digital watches and calculators to computers, use digital electronics.

Pocket calculators contain digital electronic circuits.

DIGITAL CIRCUITS

In a **digital circuit**, the electricity exists in pulses at either high voltage* or low voltage. Tiny electronic components* change and redirect these pulses as they flow around the circuits.

In an analog circuit, electricity flows continuously.

In a digital circuit, the electricity is broken up into a series of pulses.

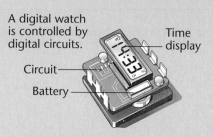

A digital watch is controlled by digital circuits.

Time display

Circuit

Battery

The pulses of electricity can be used to represent information in **binary code**. This expresses information using numbers made up of the digits 0 and 1. Words, sounds and pictures can be translated into binary, too. As there are only two options (0 and 1), devices that use digital electronics can process information very quickly.

Wave form of digital current

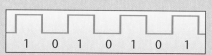

| 1 | 0 | 1 | 0 | 1 | 0 | 1 |

A pulse at high voltage represents a 1 and a pulse at low voltage represents a 0.

LOGIC GATES

A **logic gate** is an arrangement of transistors* used to carry out calculations in digital electronic circuits. Logic gates change or redirect the pulses that flow through them. Most logic gates have two **inputs**, which receive signals, and one **output**, which gives out a signal.

There are three main types of logic gates, and they are each represented by a different circuit symbol, as shown below.

AND gate	Input	Output
	1 1	1
An AND gate gives out a 1 if it receives two 1s. Otherwise, it gives out a 0.	0 1	0
	0 0	0

NOT gate	Input	Output
	1	0
A NOT gate has one input and one output. It changes a 1 to a 0 and a 0 to a 1.	0	1

OR gate	Input	Output
	1 0	1
An OR gate gives out a 1 if it receives a 1 in either of its inputs.	1 1	1
	0 0	0 ★

Logic gates have many uses. For example, an AND gate might be used in a security system, such as that used in a bank, where two officials must turn keys at the same time to open a safe. Only when both keys are turned would two 1s pass through the AND gate, and so open the lock.

This security circuit uses an AND gate so that the lock only opens when keys X and Y are both turned.

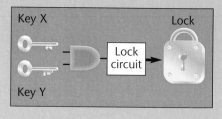

If the output is 1, current flows through the lock circuit and the lock opens.

FLIP-FLOPS

Logic gates are usually combined to make up more complex devices, such as **flip-flops**. Electric pulses circulate back and forth inside flip-flops in a process called **feedback**. This enables the flip-flops to "remember" pieces of binary information.

Integrated circuits in computers (see opposite) often contain many thousands of flip-flops. These are joined together to make the computer's memory.

Electronic components, Transistors, 43; Voltage, 36.

INTEGRATED CIRCUITS

An **integrated circuit**, also known as a **silicon chip** or **chip**, is a complete electronic circuit containing thousands of tiny components etched on a very small piece of an element called silicon.

Large cylinders of silicon are sliced into thin sections called **wafers**, and the tiny circuits are printed onto them. The wafer is then cut up with a diamond saw to make the individual chips.

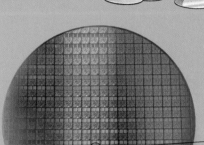

To make chips, silicon cylinders are sliced into thin wafers.

Many circuits are printed onto each wafer. The wafer is then cut up into individual chips.

This is a **CPU** (**Central Processing Unit**) chip, the main chip in a computer. It contains more than 28 million tiny transistors arranged into logic gates. The transistors are connected to each other by extremely fine aluminum threads.

Silicon is used because it is a **semiconductor** – a type of material that acts as a conductor* or an insulator*, depending on its temperature. The components that make up the circuits are also semiconductors, made of silicon mixed with tiny amounts of elements such as phosphorus or boron.

When the chips are made, they are mounted in plastic fittings which have wire feet to attach them to other components on a circuit board.

Wire feet link chips to other components.

The main circuit board in a computer is called the **motherboard**. It is made up of a piece of plastic with chips fixed onto it. The chips are connected by metal tracks printed onto the motherboard. Other components on the board control the amount of electricity flowing through the chips.

Smaller board, called a **daughterboard**, slots into the motherboard.

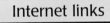

Motherboard

Internet links

• Go to **www.usborne-quicklinks.com** for a link to the **Beakman & Jax Web pages** to see how a remote control works and find out how binary numbers are used.

• Go to **www.usborne-quicklinks.com** for a link to the **Lucent Technologies Web site** to find out all about transistors.

• Go to **www.usborne-quicklinks.com** for links to the **Intel Web pages** to try out activites, watch animations and follow step-by-step explanations of how transistors work and silicon chips are made.

• Go to **www.usborne-quicklinks.com** for a link to the **PBS Web site** to learn about the first ever commercial silicon chip.

• Go to **www.usborne-quicklinks.com** for a link to the **BrainPop Web site** to find a movie and quiz about the binary code.

• Go to **www.usborne-quicklinks.com** for a link to the **Digital Logic Web site** where you can find out about logic gates.

* Conductor, Insulator, 34.

COMPUTERS

At their most basic, **computers** are machines that do calculations and sort information. When they were invented in the late 1940s, computers were so big they filled whole rooms. Since then, they have been continuously improved and made smaller. Today, computers with more power than the early ones are no bigger than this book.

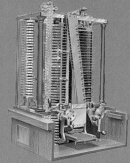

The Analytical Engine, a forerunner of the computer, built over a hundred years ago.

HARDWARE

The pieces that make up a computer are called **hardware**. Items of hardware that sit outside the case containing the computer's main electronic circuits are called **peripherals**. The screen, keyboard and mouse are all peripherals.

The type of computer shown below is called a **personal computer**, or **PC**.

This computer has a cathode ray tube* screen. It makes a picture in a similar way to a television.

Portable computers, called **laptops**, and handheld computers, called **palmtops**, have flat screens. They contain a thin layer of liquid crystal solution, which darkens to form an image when an electric current passes through it.

The keyboard is laid out like an old-fashioned typewriter, but it has some extra keys, called **function keys**. These make the computer do certain tasks.

With the mouse, you move a pointer around the screen and click on instructions. This can be quicker than using the keyboard.

SOFTWARE

A computer won't work unless it has a set of instructions called a **program**, or **software**, loaded into its memory. Software that controls how the computer works is called the **operating system**. Windows®, made by Microsoft®, is an operating system.

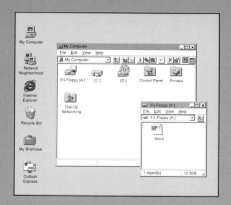

This screen shows files containing Windows software and documents.

Further software is needed to let you use the computer for particular activities such as playing games or connecting to the Internet.

Flat screen

Case contains computer's main circuits.

Mouse

Keyboard. Function keys are lined up across the top.

See for yourself

When you start up a PC, watch for lines of information which flash past your eyes. This is the computer checking through its own hardware and software, making sure that everything is working correctly.

*Cathode ray tube, 33.

This stream of 0s and 1s gives an artist's impression of how digital information flows through a computer.

BITS AND BYTES

Computers do all their calculations using a code of only two numbers: 0 and 1. This is known as **binary code**. Each 0 or 1 is called a **bit** (short for **b**inary dig**it**). Binary code is easy to express by pulses of high (1) or low (0) electrical voltage through the computer's circuits.

A group of eight bits, called a **byte**, is used to represent a small piece of data (information). Lots and lots of bytes together can represent complex data.

`01000010`

This byte stands for the keyboard letter B.

PROCESSING

Calculations in a computer are done by **microprocessors**. In a personal computer, the most important is called the **central processing unit**, or **CPU**. CPUs can deal with several million calculations per second.

A microprocessor

Bytes travel around a computer along tiny electronic pathways, called **buses**. These take information between the CPU and other parts of the computer.

PROCESSING SPEED

How quickly a microprocessor can deal with information depends on two things:

- the number of bytes that it can process at once, called **bandwidth**;

- the number of instructions it can deal with in one second, called **clock speed**. This is measured in megahertz (MHz). A CPU that can process 500,000 calculations per second is said to have a clock speed of 500MHz.

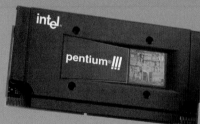

A CPU microprocessor made by Intel

Computer CDs look just like music CDs. All CDs store information in a similar way.

MEMORY

A computer stores information in its **memory**, on a set of disks called the **hard disk**. This information is retained when the computer is switched off. Information can also be stored for later use, or moved between computers, on cassette tapes, floppy disks or CDs.

A computer's **RAM (random access memory)** stores data on silicon chips* while other calculations are done by the CPU. RAM is emptied when the computer is shut down.

A floppy disk can hold a small quantity of data.

CDs can hold 450 times more information than floppy disks.

Internet links

• Go to **www.usborne-quicklinks.com** for a link to the **Kids and Computers Web site** where you can find a fun introduction to computers.

• Go to **www.usborne-quicklinks.com** for a link to the **Exploratorium Web site** to discover what's inside a floppy disc.

• Go to **www.usborne-quicklinks.com** for a link to the **BrainPop Web site** where you can watch a fun movie that explains how a computer mouse works.

• Go to **www.usborne-quicklinks.com** for a link to the **25 Years of the Microprocessor Web site** to find out about the history of the microprocessor.

• Go to **www.usborne-quicklinks.com** for a link to the **PBS People and Discoveries Web site** to read an article about the personal computer industry.

* Silicon chip, 45.

SOFTWARE PACKAGES

There are hundreds of different types of software available. These range from simple programs that let you type letters, to super-sophisticated packages that are used to design modern jets.

This picture of an Airbus was made using design software only. When the image was created, no real versions had been built.

There is software available for almost every type of work. In advertising and publishing, for instance, graphics software is used to manipulate pictures to create special effects.

Scanning this photo converted it into a mass of tiny squares, called **pixels**. Using graphics software, the pixels were altered to give the result on the right.

Close-up of pixels

Software comes loaded on floppy disks or, if it takes up a lot of memory, on CDs. These are downloaded (copied) onto the computer's hard disk.

See for yourself

Windows® contains simple graphics software called Paint®. Although it is not as powerful as the software used to create the images on these pages, you can use it to alter an image's colors and shapes.

A color-selection panel from Paint®

HARDWARE CONTROL

How a piece of computer hardware, such as the screen, works is controlled by a set of microprocessors held on a small printed circuit board called a **card**.

A graphics card controls how pictures appear on the screen.

Each card slots into the computer's main circuit board. It is controlled in turn by software called a **driver**, which needs to be installed on the computer's hard disk.

You can often improve the performance of a computer by removing a card and installing a better one, and loading a new driver into the computer. This is called **upgrading**.

HOW THIS PICTURE WAS CREATED

This picture of a snowboarder was created using graphics software on a computer with a high-quality graphics card. First of all, the photo on the far left was scanned into the computer using a scanner (see opposite page).

Using the software, background colors were changed to make it more eye-catching. The snowboarder's left hand doesn't appear in the original photo, so the right hand was copied, reversed and added to the left arm. The picture was made to look blurred to give the impression of movement.

To make the background, lines were drawn in shades of yellow and orange. They were then mixed to create a spiral effect, before the figure was placed on top.

EXTRA HARDWARE

As well as basic hardware such as a screen, keyboard and mouse, other peripherals can be attached to a computer. These include printers, scanners and devices such as CD recorders for storing lots of information.

Speakers let you listen to music or speech on software, or downloaded from the Internet.

This steering wheel and foot pedal attach to the computer and make computer driving games more realistic and exciting.

A scanner turns text and pictures into digital information which can be stored in the computer.

How a scanner works

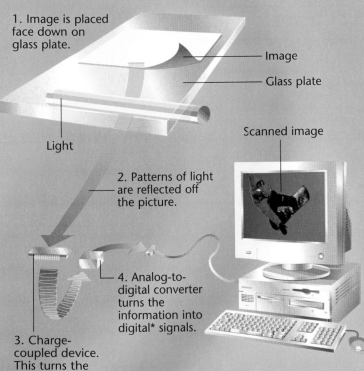

1. Image is placed face down on glass plate.

Image

Glass plate

Light

Scanned image

2. Patterns of light are reflected off the picture.

3. Charge-coupled device. This turns the light patterns into analog* electrical signals.

4. Analog-to-digital converter turns the information into digital* signals.

5. Digital signals are sent along a cable to the computer.

NETWORKS

Connecting computers to each other is called **networking**. It allows information to be shared easily. A network can consist of computers that are close to each other or thousands of miles apart.

A network consisting of computers that are close together, for example all in the same room, is called a **local-area network**, or **LAN**.

The simplest LAN consists of just two computers in the same room.

A network of computers that are far apart is called a **wide-area network**, or **WAN**.

A WAN can join computers anywhere in the world.

TYPES OF NETWORKS

The simplest kind of network is called **peer-to-peer**. This means that the network is not controlled by any one computer. Peer-to-peer networks are fairly easy to set up.

★

A peer-to-peer network setup

In **client/server** networks, one computer, called the **server**, has control of the network. Important programs and data are held on the server. Other computers (the **clients**) collect these from the server to work on. If the server is not working, the clients can't use the data, so the network doesn't function.

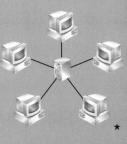

★

A client/server network setup

Client/server networks can process more information than peer-to-peer networks.

Internet links

• Go to **www.usborne-quicklinks.com** for a link to the **BrainPop Web site** to find a friendly introduction to computers.

• Go to **www.usborne-quicklinks.com** for a link to the **Virtual Computer History Museum Group Web site** where you can find facts and images about the history of the computer.

• Go to **www.usborne-quicklinks.com** for a link to **Michelle Hoyle's Web site** to learn all about computers from the past to the present, by exploring a fascinating series of slides and diagrams.

* Analog, Digital, 44.

TELECOMS

Since the invention of the telephone in 1876, there have been continual improvements to telephone systems. Used with computers, there is now a whole range of ways that people can send and receive information. This branch of technology is called **telecommunications**, or **telecoms**.

This telephone handset is attached by a cord to its base unit. Cordless phones communicate with their base unit using radio waves.

TELEPHONE LINES

Traditionally, telephone messages are carried by cables made of copper that are either buried underground or slung between poles.

Originally, these cables carried analog* signals generated by the telephone. Many modern telephones send and receive digital information, which needs less power and takes up less room on the cable. As a result, more information can pass along the lines.

Satellite

Radio-signal transmitter masts

TELEPHONE SYSTEM

The **telephone system** consists of a complicated network of cables, switches and telephone exchanges.

If you make a long-distance call, your message may be bounced off a satellite in outer space, beamed between transmitter masts, or simply routed through huge lengths of cabling. Whichever route it takes, your call will reach its destination in a matter of seconds.

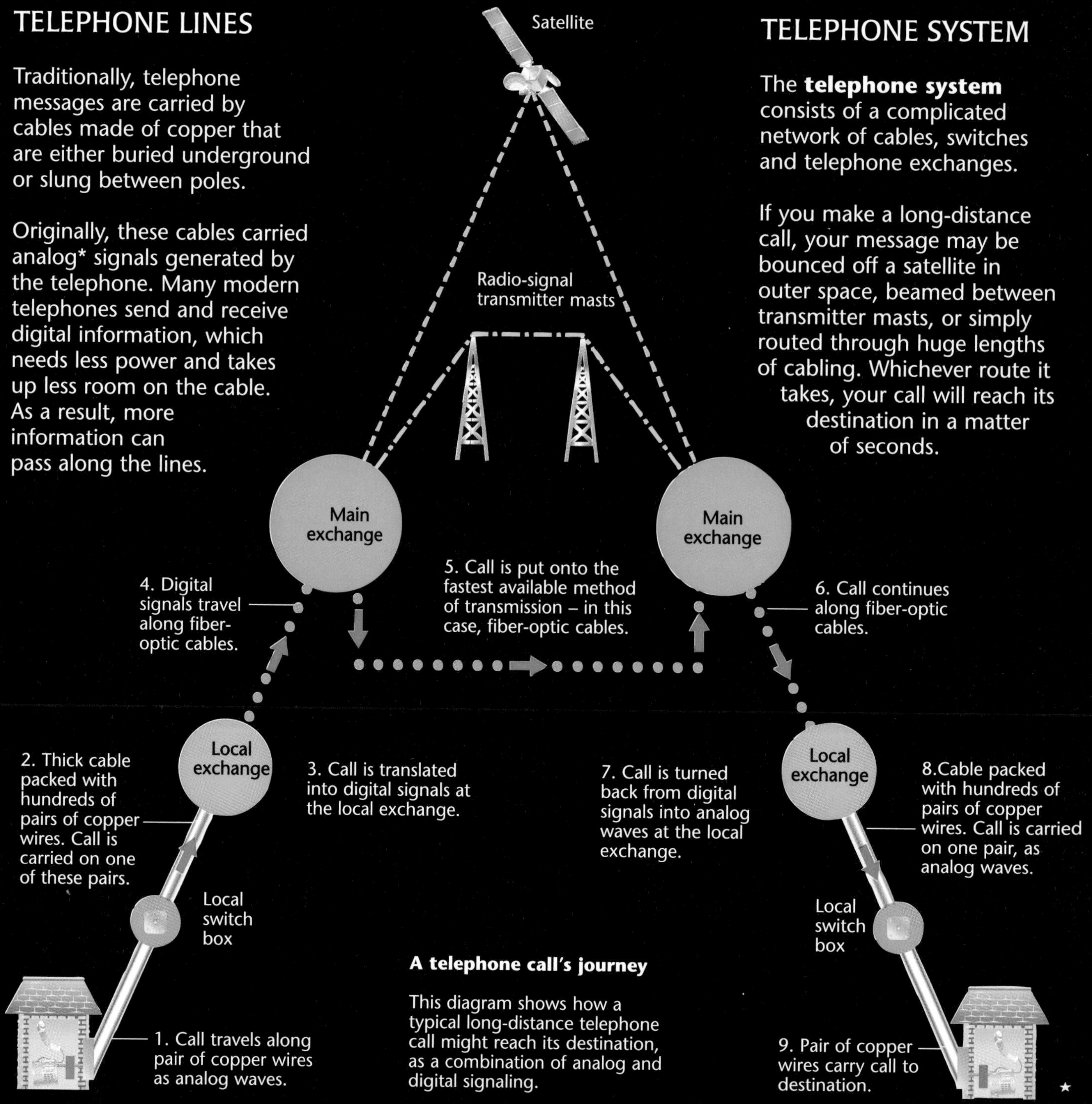

Main exchange

Main exchange

4. Digital signals travel along fiber-optic cables.

5. Call is put onto the fastest available method of transmission – in this case, fiber-optic cables.

6. Call continues along fiber-optic cables.

Local exchange

Local exchange

2. Thick cable packed with hundreds of pairs of copper wires. Call is carried on one of these pairs.

3. Call is translated into digital signals at the local exchange.

7. Call is turned back from digital signals into analog waves at the local exchange.

8. Cable packed with hundreds of pairs of copper wires. Call is carried on one pair, as analog waves.

Local switch box

Local switch box

A telephone call's journey

This diagram shows how a typical long-distance telephone call might reach its destination, as a combination of analog and digital signaling.

1. Call travels along pair of copper wires as analog waves.

9. Pair of copper wires carry call to destination.

★

50

Analog, 44.

MODEMS

A **modem** allows a computer or fax to send and receive information along telephone lines. "Modem" stands for **mo**dulator-**dem**odulator.

The modem converts, or modulates, digital information produced by a computer or fax into analog waves. The modem receiving the information demodulates (turns back) the waves into digital code which is understood by another computer or fax.

Modem

TRANSMISSION SPEED

The amount of information that can be sent by a modem is limited by the speed at which it can process information. **Data compression** can speed this up by cutting out any information that is not vital.

For example, music can be compressed using **mp3** software. This removes parts of sound that your ears can't detect. A stripped-down version is left, which is quicker to send.

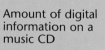

Amount of digital information on a music CD

Amount of digital information after mp3 compression

Mp3 software cuts out any very high or very low frequency soundwaves that are out of the range of sounds that you can hear. It also cuts out sounds that are masked by other sounds.

BANDWIDTH

The amount of information that can be processed each second by a telephone line is called its **bandwidth**. Copper cabling has a limited bandwidth. **Fiber-optic cables**, made of glass or plastic fibers, have a much greater bandwidth. However, they are expensive to install.

MOBILE PHONES

Mobile telephones do not make use of telephone lines. Instead, they send digital radio signals through the air to nearby transmitter masts, called **base stations**. These pass the signal on to the next station, and on and on, until they reach the phone that you are calling.

How a mobile phone works

1. You dial a number and press the call key.

2. Your phone chooses an available radio channel and sends a digital radio signal of the phone number to the nearest base station.

Radio signal

Transmitter mast, or base station

3. The base station sends the signal around the network of base stations, until it finds the phone you are calling.

4. The phone you are calling sends a message back via the base stations, saying whether it is available. Only now do you hear a ringing tone.

Here you can see light shining out of the ends of a bundle of fiber-optic cables. Fiber-optic cables carry digital information as pulses of light.

See for yourself

Try dialing a fax number from a telephone. When the fax answers your call, you will hear a high-pitched warbling sound. This is its internal modem sending a little message. The message is to establish whether a fax is calling it, and if so, to tell the other fax to start transmitting its information.

Internet links

• Go to **www.usborne-quicklinks.com** for a link to the **AT&T Web site** to play interactive games and discover fascinating facts about the telephone, its history, and its technological development.

• Go to **www.usborne-quicklinks.com** for a link to the **PBS Web site** to try a radio transmission activity, or learn about the history and science of radios.

• Go to **www.usborne-quicklinks.com** for links to the **BrainPop Web pages** to watch fun movies and play quizzes about TV and radio.

• Go to **www.usborne-quicklinks.com** for links to the **How Stuff Works Web pages** to find easy-to-read explanations of how telephones and cell phones work, illustrated by amazing animations.

THE INTERNET

The **Internet** is a vast computer network linking together millions of computers all over the world. It gives access to information put onto it by individuals, companies and organizations. The Internet can also be used to exchange information, send messages and to buy things.

1. You log on to the Internet via your phone line.

2. The message that you type into your computer's browser goes to your ISP.

INTERNET BASICS

Most people connect, or **log on**, to the Internet using software called a **browser**.

The basic structure of the Internet is provided by telephone companies. Their phone lines carry the information that you send and receive when you use the Internet.

Most home users use **Internet service providers** (**ISPs**) to access the Internet. When you are **online** (connected to the Internet) messages go from your computer down the phone line to the ISP's powerful computers. The computers work like electronic post offices, automatically sorting and sending things on in a matter of seconds.

The World Wide Web is the most well-known, and most widely used, part of the Internet.

6. The ISP sends the information back to your computer down the phone line.

ISP

Router

3. Your ISP sends the message on, via a series of powerful computers called **routers**.

4. The information is passed on until it reaches the computer that holds the information, called a **server**.

Router

5. The server sends the information that you asked for back to the ISP via routers.

Server

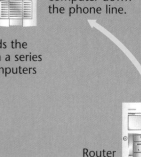

WORLD WIDE WEB

The **World Wide Web** (**www**) is a huge information resource and a place to conduct e-commerce (see opposite page). It consists of thousands of individual Web sites. Each site is made up of individual documents, called Web pages.

HTML

Web pages are written using a computer language called **HyperText Markup Language** (**HTML**). If you are looking at a Web page, you can view the HTML code by clicking on the "View" button and then choosing "Source".

HYPERLINKS

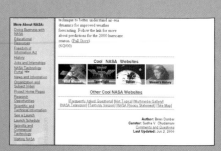

On Web pages, some words or pictures are highlighted. Click on them and a new page with related information is shown, or **downloaded**. This is a **hyperlink**. These links enable you to jump really quickly from page to page all over the Web.

INTERNET NAMES

Each piece of information on the Internet has an address, called a **URL** (**Uniform Resource Locator**). A URL enables you to call up the exact piece of information you want. It also defines the format (called the **protocol**) in which the messages are sent.

A URL

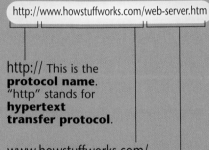

http://www.howstuffworks.com/web-server.htm

http:// This is the **protocol name**. "http" stands for **hypertext transfer protocol**.

www.howstuffworks.com/ is the **domain name**. This identifies the name of the site and the Web server it is held on.

web-server.htm is the **file path**. This is the name of the file in which the page is stored. The *.htm* part shows that the file is written in HTML code.

DOT COM

The final part of a domain name is called the **top-level domain**. Here are some examples and what they indicate:

.com - commercial organization
.edu - school or educational establishment
.gov - government agency
.org - non-profit organization (such as a charity)

Some domain names have an extra two letters to identify which country they are based in. For example:

.es - Spain
.th - Thailand
.uk - United Kingdom

E-MAIL

E-mail stands for **electronic mail**. It is a way of using your computer to send messages to other Internet users. You write and read e-mails using special e-mail software, such as Outlook Express®, made by Microsoft®.

E-mail is sent down the phone line to your ISP. It is sent on to the recipient's ISP via the Internet, where it waits for delivery the next time the recipient logs on to the Internet.

E-mail addresses have three parts. Here's a typical one:

joeschmo@slugpost.com

joeschmo is the name that the person has decided to use when sending and receiving e-mails.

@ stands for "at".

slugpost.com is the domain name. For home computer users, this is normally the name of your ISP.

E-COMMERCE

The Internet can be used to buy and sell things. This is called **e-commerce**. Goods and services that are offered for sale on a Web site can be ordered directly by filling in an order form which appears on the Web page.

E-commerce enables people to shop for just about anything, at any time, and from anywhere. However, it means that you can't inspect the goods or try them out before you buy.

MOBILE INTERNET

There is a part of the Internet that can be accessed by some mobile telephones. It displays Web pages that are written in a different protocol and have few pictures. The pages are simpler than regular Internet pages because mobile phone lines can't carry the amount of digital information contained in a regular Web page quickly enough.

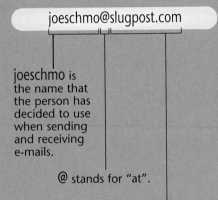

You can access the Internet and send e-mails from this mobile phone.

See for yourself

To see just how quickly e-mail zips from place to place, try sending yourself an e-mail. Write your own address in the "To:" window and then click "Send". (You don't need to add a subject name, even if the e-mail software asks for one.)

The e-mail should come back from your ISP (which could be in another country) in seconds. However, it may take longer, depending on how busy the Internet is at the time.

Internet links

• Go to **www.usborne-quicklinks.com** for a link to the **How Stuff Works Web site** to find easy-to-read explanations of how different features of the Internet work.

• Go to **www.usborne-quicklinks.com** for a link to the **AT&T Web site** to find a great introduction to the internet.

• Go to **www.usborne-quicklinks.com** for a link to the **Beakman & Jax Web pages** where you can find an interactive demonstration of how the Internet works.

• Go to **www.usborne-quicklinks.com** for a link to the **BrainPop Web site** to watch a movie about the Internet.

• Go to **www.usborne-quicklinks.com** for a link to the **PBS People and Discoveries Web site** for an article about the Internet and the World Wide Web.

FACTS AND LISTS

ELECTRICAL AND ELECTRONIC SYMBOLS

The symbols below are used to represent components found in electrical and electronic circuits. Different countries sometimes use alternative symbols.

Wire	AC source	Transistor	Ammeter
Wires crossed	Bulb	Microphone	Voltmeter
Wires connected	Fuse	Loudspeaker	Integrated electrical circuit (chip)
Switch	Capacitor	Bell	Negative polarity
Terminals	Diode	Amplifier	Positive polarity
Connection to earth	Light-emitting diode	NOT gate	Magnetic field lines
Single cell. (Long line is + terminal, short line is – terminal.)	Resistor	AND gate	Antenna
Multi-cell battery	Variable resistor	OR gate	
	Thermistor		

LAWS AND EQUATIONS

The following equations apply to various aspects of an electrical circuit.

Current is equal to voltage divided by resistance ($I = V/R$)
Power is equal to voltage multiplied by current ($P = VI$)

SI units

SI units (short for *Système Internationale d'Unites*) are an internationally agreed system of very precise units used for scientific purposes. There are seven basic units, but more can be derived using equations (see below).

Quantity	SI unit
Time	second (s)
Current	Ampere (A)
Temperature	kelvin (K)
Length	meter (m)
Mass	kilogram (kg)
Light intensity	candela (cd)
Amount of a substance	mole (mol)

Quantity	Equation	Derived SI unit
Electric charge	Current (A) x time (s)	coulomb (C)
Voltage	$\dfrac{\text{Energy transferred (J)}}{\text{Charge (C)}}$	volt (V)
Resistance	$\dfrac{\text{Voltage (V)}}{\text{Current (A)}}$	ohm (Ω)

BINARY NUMBERS

The binary system used in computers represents letters and numbers as a series of 1s and 0s. Here are the numbers one to ten represented in binary code.

Decimal	Binary
1	1
2	10
3	11
4	100
5	101
6	110
7	111
8	1000
9	1001
10	1010

Binary on the Web

Go to *www.usborne-quicklinks.com* for Web sites which provide a thorough and interesting guide to binary, and information on how to count in binary using your fingers.

HISTORY OF THE COMPUTER

Over the last century, the development of computers has affected the lives of people all over the world. In a relatively short time, huge advances have been made in this field, including the creation of the home computer and the rise of the Internet. On this page, you will find a brief history of the computer industry. For further information on this topic, visit the Web sites described on page 45.

1642 Blaise Pascal invents the Pascaline computer, the first mechanical calculator. The principles it operated on are still used in modern odometers (devices for measuring distance traveled by a bicycle or motor vehicle).

1822 Charles Babbage invents the Difference Engine, the forerunner of the modern computer. However, the huge, steam-powered machine never passed the prototype stage.

1830 Charles Babbage invents the Analytical Engine (see p.45), a more sophisticated machine than the Difference Engine.

1890 First use of punched cards to store large amounts of data, a method which continued to be used well into the 1940s. Herman Hollerith, the pioneer of this system, founded the company which would later become the modern IBM.

1937 Alan Turing creates plans for a sophisticated computer which became known as the "Turing Machine".

1941 Konrad Zuse completes the first fully-functioning electro-mechanical computer, called the Z3. It operated on a binary sytem, using holes punched in strips of tape.

1943 The first electronic digital computer, called the ENIAC (Electrical Numerical Integrator and Computer), is created. It was 1,000 times faster than any computer before it.

1945 Von Neumann develops the stored program technique, enabling programs to be stored with data in the computer's memory. This new technology allows the first commercial computers, called the EDVAC and UNIVAC, to be built in the late 1940s. This is known as the "first generation" of computers.

1947 Invention of the transistor by William Shockley, John Bardeen, and Walter Brattain of Bell Labs. This gives rise to the "second generation" of computers, which are much smaller than first generation machines.

1958 Jack Kilby builds the first integrated circuit (chip), made up of many tiny transistors. As a result, even more compact "third generation" computers are created.

1964 John Kemeny and Thomas Kurtz develop BASIC (Beginners All-purpose Symbolic Instruction Code), an easy-to-learn programming language.

1971 Intel builds the first microprocessor, the Intel 4004. The "fourth generation" of computers is created.

1972 The games industry is born as Atari creates the first commercial video game, "Pong".

1975 The first general use microcomputer, the Altair, becomes available in home-assembly kit form. It had a 256 byte memory and required the user to write their own software. Bill Gates and Paul Allen, who would later found Microsoft®, developed BASIC for use on this system.

1976 Steve Jobs and Steve Wozniak form the Apple Computer Company. The Apple II home computer goes on sale.

1977 IBM begins work on the Acorn home computer. This later becomes the IBM PC.

1981 IBM releases the IBM PC, the first general use computer for home, schools and offices. As a result, the number of personal computer users increases from 2 million in 1981 to 5.5 million in 1982.

1984 The Apple Macintosh is introduced. This is the first home computer with a graphical user interface or GUI (an operating system based on icons rather than text) and a mouse. The 3.5" floppy disk is introduced and soon becomes the industry standard.

1985 Microsoft® launches the Windows® 1.0 operating system.

1986 IBM release the first true laptop computer, the IBM PC Convertible.

1987 Microsoft® releases the Excel® spreadsheet program and Word® 4.0 for Windows®.

1989 Tim Berner-Lee develops the World Wide Web.

1991 The CERN lab creates the first Web server.

1994 Two Web browsers, Netscape Navigator 1.0 and Microsoft Internet Explorer® 3.0, are released.

2001 Number of Internet users worldwide has grown from 3 million in 1994 to an estimated 407 million.

SCIENTISTS AND INVENTORS

al-Haytham, Ibn (Alhazen) (965-1038) An Arab physicist who made great advances in optics, explaining refraction, and the role of reflection in vision.

Ampère, André Marie (1775-1836) A French mathematician and physicist who did pioneering work on electricity and magnetism. The unit of electric current, called the ampere, is named after him.

Babbage, Charles (1792-1871) An English mathematician and inventor who worked on a calculating machine called the Analytical Engine, a forerunner of the modern computer.

Baird, John Logie (1888-1946) A Scottish engineer who invented the television in 1926.

Bell, Alexander Graham (1847-1922) A Scottish-American inventor who invented the telephone (1872-76).

Berliner, Émile (1851-1929) This German-American engineer invented the gramophone.

Edison, Thomas (1847-1931) This American inventor made over a thousand devices including the phonograph, an early version of the gramophone.

Faraday, Michael (1791-1867) An English scientist who invented the dynamo, generating an electric current by spinning a coil of wire in a magnetic field.

Franklin, Benjamin (1706-1790) This American inventor and politician proved that lightning is a form of electricity.

Gilbert, William (1544-1603) This English physicist, also doctor to Queen Elizabeth I of England, founded the scientific study of magnetism. He was the first to suggest that the Earth is magnetic.

Hertz, Heinrich (1857-1894) This German physicist began the research that demonstrated the existence of radio waves.

Lovelace, Ada (1815-1852) An English mathematician, Lovelace worked on the Analytical Engine designed by Charles Babbage, devising "programs" which anticipated computer programming.

Maiman, Theodore (1927-) An American scientist who built the first laser.

Marconi, Guglielmo (1874-1937) This Italian physicist developed radiotelegraphy and succeeded in sending signals across the Atlantic in 1901.

Morse, Samuel (1791-1872) An American artist who invented a system of sending messages along electric telegraph wires by a coded system of dots and dashes (long and short electrical pulses) now called Morse code.

Newton, Isaac (1642-1727) This English physicist and mathematician formulated fundamental laws of gravity and motion. He also discovered that light is made up of a spectrum of colors, and built the first reflecting telescope.

Ohm, Georg (1787-1854) A German physicist who researched electrical resistance. The SI unit of electrical resistance, called the ohm, is named after him.

Pascal, Blaise (1623-1662) A French mathematician and physicist who made contributions to hydraulics and the study of atmospheric pressure. The SI unit of pressure, called the pascal, is named after him.

Röntgen, Wilhelm (1845-1923) This German physicist discovered X-rays in 1895.

Ruska, Ernst (1906-1988) A German engineer who invented the electron microscope in 1933.

Talbot, William Fox (1800-1877) This British scientist invented the method of reproducing photographs from a negative image.

Tesla, Nikola (1856-1943) A Croatian electrical engineer who invented the AC motor and high-voltage electrical generation.

Turing, Alan (1912-1954) This English mathematician was an important pioneer of computer science.

Villard, Paul (1860-1934) A French physicist who discovered gamma radiation in 1900.

Volta, Alessandro (1745-1827) An Italian physicist who built the first electric battery. The volt, which measures electric potential, is named after him.

Watt, James (1736-1819) A Scottish inventor who improved the steam engine and introduced the sun-and-planet gear. The watt, the SI unit of electrical power (equivalent to one joule per second), is named after him.

TEST YOURSELF

1. All waves are:
A. vibrations and carry energy
B. vibrations in the same direction as the wave is traveling
C. vibrations at right angles to the direction the wave is traveling
(Pages 8-9)

2. The wavelength of a wave is:
A. the number of complete waves that pass a point in one second
B. the distance between a peak and the next trough
C. the distance between a peak and the next peak
(Page 9)

3. When a wave hits a surface and bounces off, it is:
A. reflected
B. refracted
C. diffracted
(Pages 10-11)

4. When a wave enters a new medium at an angle and changes direction, it is:
A. reflected
B. refracted
C. diffracted
(Pages 10-11)

5. Sound waves:
A. are electromagnetic waves
B. can travel through a vacuum
C. travel more quickly in solids than in gases
(Pages 8, 12-13)

6. Sound waves in air:
A. always travel at the same speed
B. cannot be reflected off obstacles
C. are made up of vibrations of the air molecules
(Pages 12-13)

7. The loudness of a note from a stringed instrument is increased by:
A. plucking the string harder
B. lengthening the string
C. shortening the string
(Page 14)

8. The pitch of a note from a stringed instrument is raised by:
A. plucking the string harder
B. lengthening the string
C. shortening the string
(Page 15)

9. Ultraviolet rays:
A. have a shorter wavelength than visible light
B. travel faster than visible light
C. have a longer wavelength than visible light
(Page 18)

10. Light cannot pass through:
A. transparent objects
B. translucent objects
C. opaque objects
(Page 20)

11. The penumbra is the:
A. area where all the light falls
B. dark area of a shadow
C. gray area of a shadow
(Page 20)

12. Which statement is not true?
A. white light can be split up into its various colors using a prism
B. blue light is refracted the least
C. different colors are refracted by different amounts
(Page 22)

13. Red, green and blue light are:
A. primary colors
B. secondary colors
C. complementary colors
(Page 22)

14. When red light and blue light are mixed, the resulting color is:
A. blue
B. red
C. magenta
(Page 22)

15. When white light falls on a blue object, the object appears:
A. blue
B. white
C. black
(Page 23)

16. Light interference happens when light rays:
A. travel parallel to each other
B. travel in opposite directions
C. cross
(Page 25)

17. Polarized sunglasses reduce the glare in your eyes because they:
A. filter out all light wave vibrations that are not in a certain direction
B. reflect light away from your eyes
C. bend light so that it does not all reach your eyes
(Page 25)

18. A glass bi-convex lens in air:
A. has surfaces which curve inward
B. acts as a converging lens
C. acts as a diverging lens
(Page 26)

19. A short-sighted person:
A. cannot see nearby objects clearly
B. cannot see distant objects clearly
C. needs glasses with converging lenses
(Page 27)

20. Small objects look larger using a:
A. microscope
B. periscope
C. telescope
(Page 28)

21. The aperture of a camera controls:
A. how much light enters the camera
B. the time that light falls on the film
C. the size of the image
(Page 30)

22. Two charged particles attract one another when:
A. both are positively charged
B. both are negatively charged
C. one is positively charged and the other negatively charged
(Page 34)

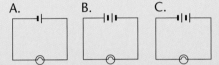

23. Which diagram correctly shows a circuit with two single cells, with the positive terminals to the right, connected to a bulb?
(Page 54)

24. The diagram on the right shows a bulb, two single cells and a:
A. resistor
B. transistor
C. diode
(Page 54)

25. Which of the following magnetic poles will attract each other?
A. a north and a north
B. a north and a south
C. a south and a south
(Page 38)

26. Soft ferromagnetic materials are:
A. easy to magnetize and demagnetize
B. hard to magnetize and demagnetize
C. used to make permanent magnets
(Page 38)

27. A machine which converts energy of movement into electrical energy is:
A. a generator
B. a motor
C. an armature
(Page 41)

28. If the resistance of an electrical component in a series circuit increases, then the current:
A. is increased
B. is reduced
C. stays the same
(Pages 36, 42)

Answers

1.A 2.C 3.A 4.B 5.C 6.C 7.A 8.C 9.A 10.C 11.C 12.B 13.A 14.C 15.A 16.C 17.A 18.B 19.B 20.A 21.B 22.C 23.C 24.A 25.B 26.A 27.A 28.B

57

A-Z OF SCIENTIFIC TERMS

AC See *alternating current*.
accumulator See *secondary cell*.
achromatic colors Black, white and the shades of gray in between.
acoustic wave See *sound wave*.
additive mixing The process of adding different combinations of red, green and blue light to make light of almost any color.
alternating current (**AC**) Electric current that changes direction many times a second.
AM See *amplitude modulation*.
ammeter A device used to measure electric current.
ampere (**A**) The SI unit of electric current.
amplify To make something greater, for example, to increase the loudness of a sound.
amplitude The maximum displacement of particles in a wave from their rest position. It is the distance from a peak to the rest position on a wave diagram.
amplitude modulation (**AM**) A type of modulation where the amplitude of the carrier wave is altered to match the sound and picture signals being carried.
analog The term that describes a continuous signal which varies in proportion to the quantity it represents.
aperture On a camera, the adjustable hole which, together with the shutter, controls the exposure.
armature A rotating coil in an electric motor.

bandwidth The number of bytes a microprocessor can process at once.
base station A mast used to transmit digital radio signals between mobile phones.
battery A source of electrical potential energy made up of one or more electrochemical cells.
binary code A method used to represent information using the digits 1 and 0.
bit (**binary digit**) A single piece of information in binary code – a 0 or a 1.
browser Computer software used to log on to the Internet.
buses Electronic pathways that carry information between the CPU and the other parts of a computer.
byte A group of eight bits of information.

candela (**cd**) The SI unit of light intensity.
capacitor An electronic component which stores up electrical energy until it is needed. Capacitance is measured in farads (F).

carrier waves See *modulation*.
cathode ray tube A glass tube, containing a vacuum, which is used in television to turn picture signals into beams of electrons. These sweep across the screen to build up images.
CCD See *charge-coupled device*.
cell See *electrochemical cell*.
Central Processing Unit (**CPU**) The main integrated circuit, set of circuits or PCBs, controlling the operation of a computer.
charge-coupled device (**CCD**) A light-sensitive electronic part, found for example in a camcorder, that produces electrical signals.
chromatic colors All the colors of the visible light spectrum.
clock speed The number of instructions a microprocessor can deal with in one second, measured in **megahertz** (**MHz**).
coherent The term that describes waves that have the same wavelength and frequency and travel in step with each other.
coil See *solenoid*.
commutator A device in an electric motor that causes the direction of an electric current to be reversed.
complementary colors Any two colors that together make up white light.
compound microscope A microscope with two or more lenses.
concave Of a surface, curving inward.
conduction 1. The way heat energy is transferred in a solid by the vibration of the solid's heated particles. 2. The way an electric current is transferred in a substance by the movement of free electrons.
conductor A substance through which an electric current can flow, or heat can flow easily.
constructive interference An increase in amplitude that may result when two waves meet.
converging lens A lens that causes parallel light rays passing through it to come together.
convex Of a surface, curving outward.
coulomb (**C**) The SI unit of electric charge.
CPU See *Central Processing Unit*.

data compression Methods used to increase the speed at which data can be transmitted, by leaving out inessential information.
DC See *direct current*.
decibel (**dB**) The unit of loudness (this is related to the amplitude of sound waves).
destructive interference A decrease in amplitude that may result when two waves meet.

diaphragm The thin disc inside a microphone (or speaker) that vibrates at the same frequency as the sound waves hitting it (or the electrical signal energizing it).
diffraction The bending of a wave when it meets an obstacle or passes through a gap.
diffuse reflection Reflection in which parallel incident waves bounce off an object in many directions.
digital The term that describes a signal made up of separate electrical pulses, used to represent the 0s and 1s of binary code.
diode An electronic component which allows current to flow through it in one direction only.
dipoles (or **molecular magnets**) The molecules of a ferromagnetic material, which behave like tiny magnets.
direct current (**DC**) Electric current that flows in one direction only.
dispersion The splitting up of light into the colors of the visible light spectrum.
diverging lens A lens that causes parallel rays of light passing through it to spread out.
domain A group of dipoles, all lined up and pointing the same way, in a ferromagnetic material. When the material is magnetized, all the domains become ordered and point the same way.
dry cell A type of electrochemical cell which contains an electrolyte paste, not a liquid.
dynamo See *generator*.

earth wire A safety device in an electric cable that provides a path for the current to flow to the ground.
echo location Any method of locating an object by detecting the return of sound waves bouncing off that object, as, for example, when dolphins or bats find their way around. See also *sonar* and *ultrasound*.
electric charge A property of matter which causes electric forces between particles. Opposite charges attract, while like charges repel each other. Charge is measured in coulombs (C).
electric current A flow of electrically charged particles. Current is measured in amperes (A).
electric field The area in which an electric force has an effect.
electric force The effect that electrically charged particles have on each other.
electricity The effect caused by the presence or movement of electrically charged particles.

electric motor A device that changes electrical energy into movement.

electrochemical cell (or **cell**) A device which produces electric energy from chemical energy by the movement of charged particles in a substance called an **electrolyte**. Several cells joined together make a battery.

electromagnet A magnet (made of a solenoid with a soft ferromagnetic core) which can be switched on and off by an electric current.

electromagnetic spectrum The arrangement of electromagnetic waves in order of wavelength and frequency.

electromagnetic waves Transverse waves made up of continually changing electric and magnetic fields, for example, light.

electromagnetism The effect that takes place when an electric current flows through a wire, creating a magnetic field around the wire.

electron A negatively charged particle that moves around the nucleus (core) of an atom.

electronic circuit An electric circuit that contains electronic components.

electronic components Devices that control the flow of a current in an electronic circuit.

exposure The amount of light that is allowed in through a camera lens.

eyepiece The lens in an optical instrument that refracts light from the objective lens, and produces the final, magnified image.

Farad (**F**) The SI unit of electrical capacitance.

feedback In electronics, the process which returns part or all of an output signal to the input.

ferromagnetic The term used to describe metals that can be magnetized strongly, for example iron and steel.

fiber-optic cable A cable made up of many glass or plastic fibers, used to transmit light.

flip-flop A combination of logic gates often used to store binary information.

fluorescence The ability of certain substances to absorb ultraviolet radiation, or other forms of energy, and give it out as light.

FM See *frequency modulation*.

focus Any point where light rays come together, or appear to come from.

frequency The number of waves passing a point in one second, measured in hertz (Hz).

frequency modulation (**FM**) A type of modulation in which the frequency of the carrier wave is altered to match the sound and picture signals being carried.

fundamental frequency The main, strongest frequency in a musical note, which is the same whatever the instrument.

fuse A safety device with a thin piece of wire in it that melts and cuts off an electric current if it becomes too large.

Gamma radiation (**gamma rays**) Electromagnetic waves with the shortest wavelength and highest frequency. They are given off by radioactive substances.

generator (or **dynamo**) A machine that converts movement energy into electricity.

Hard disk A set of magnetic disks in a computer that continues to store information after the computer has been switched off.

harmonics (or **overtones**) Sound vibrations of different frequencies that mix with a note's fundamental frequency to give an instrument its timbre.

hertz (**Hz**) The SI unit of frequency.

high-fidelity recording A sound recording that is very similar to the original.

hyperlink A piece of text or picture on a Web page that links to another page when clicked on.

Incident wave (**ray**) A wave (whose direction is shown as a ray in the case of a light wave) that is traveling towards a boundary between two media.

infrared radiation (**infrared rays**) Electromagnetic waves that are given out by anything hot.

infrasound Sound waves with a frequency below 20 hertz.

insulator A substance that cannot conduct electric current, or does not conduct heat well.

integrated circuit See *silicon chip*.

intensity The level of brightness of the light given off by an object, measured in candelas (cd).

interference The effect that occurs when two or more waves meet. See *constructive interference; destructive interference*.

iridescence The effect of shimmering colors, caused by light wave interference, seen on the moving surfaces of shiny objects.

Laser (**l**ight **a**mplification by **s**timulated **e**mission of **r**adiation) A machine that creates beams of intense, pure color of one wavelength and frequency (**laser beams**).

light-emitting diode (**LED**) A diode which glows when an electric current flows through it.

live wire One of two current-carrying wires in an electric cable.

logic gate An arrangement of transistors used to carry out calculations in digital electronic circuits.

longitudinal wave A wave in which the particles vibrate in the same direction as the wave is travelling.

Magnetic field The area around a magnet in which the magnetic force has an effect.

magnetic flux lines Lines which show the direction and strength of the magnetic field around a magnet.

magnetism (**magnetic force**) An invisible force that attracts certain metals, including iron.

mechanical wave A wave made up of the vibrations of the particles of a solid, liquid or gas.

microprocessor An integrated circuit, or set of circuits, which carries out the calculations in a computer. In a personal computer, the main one is the CPU.

microwaves Radio waves with a relatively short wavelength. Used in cooking and telecommunications.

modem (**mo**dulator/**dem**odulator) A device which allows a computer to send or receive information along telephone lines.

modulation A process by which sound and picture signals are mixed with radio waves (the **carrier waves**) so they can be broadcast.

molecular magnets See *dipoles*.

Neutral wire One of two current-carrying wires in an electric cable.

Objective lens The lens in an optical instrument that refracts light from the object to form an upside-down image that looks bigger.

ohm (**Ω**) The SI unit of electrical resistance.

operating system The software that controls how a computer works.

optical instrument A device that uses combinations of lenses and mirrors to produce a particular type of image.

optical microscope An instrument that uses lenses to make small objects look bigger.

optical telescope An instrument that uses lenses and mirrors to make distant objects look closer and therefore larger.

overtones See *harmonics*.

Parallel circuit An electric circuit with more than one path through which a current can flow.

PCB See *printed circuit board*.

penumbra A pale shadow formed in an area lit by only part of a light source.

peripherals Pieces of computer hardware, such as a keyboard or mouse, that sit outside the case containing the computer's main circuits.

persistent vision The illusion of seeing movement when watching a quickly-changing series of still images, for example a movie.

pigment A substance that absorbs some colors of light and reflects others, so making an object appear colored.

pitch The highness or lowness of a sound.

pixel Short for "picture element". A tiny dot or square that forms part of a picture on a TV screen or monitor.

playback head The part of a cassette recorder that translates information stored on magnetized tape so it can be reproduced as sound.

polarized light Light in which the vibrations of electric and magnetic fields all occur in one direction only.

pole 1. An electrical terminal.
2. Either of the two ends of a magnet where the force of attraction or repulsion is strongest.

potential difference (or **voltage**) The work needed to push a certain amount of electric charge between two points on a conducting pathway. It is measured in volts (V).

primary cell Any electrochemical cell which has a limited life because the chemicals inside it are used up over time.

primary colors Colors from which all others can be made. The primary colors of light are red, green and blue. Those of pigments are magenta, yellow and cyan.

printed circuit board (**PCB**) A plastic board imprinted with metal tracks, used in electronics.

protocol In computing, the format in which messages are sent between computers.

R **adar** (**ra**dio **d**etection **a**nd **r**anging) The use of reflected microwaves to find the position of distant objects.

radio telescope A telescope which detects distant stars by collecting their radio signals.

radio waves Electromagnetic waves with the longest wavelength and the lowest frequency, including microwaves and those used for standard TV and radio broadcasting.

RAM (**R**andom **A**ccess **M**emory) The memory a computer uses while it is working, made up of integrated circuits.

recording head The part of a cassette recorder that records sounds onto the tape.

reflection The change in direction of a wave due to its bouncing off a boundary between one medium and another.

reflector telescope A telescope that uses a mirror to collect light.

refraction The change in direction of a wave due to its moving into a medium in which its speed is different.

refractor telescope A telescope that uses a lens to collect light.

regular reflection Reflection in which parallel incident waves have parallel reflected waves.

resistance The ability of a substance to reduce the flow of electric current, measured in ohms (Ω).

resistor An electronic component which reduces the flow of current.

resolution The degree of detail in an image.

resonate To vibrate in response to, and at the same frequency as, vibrations received from somewhere else.

rheostat See *variable resistor*.

S **ampling** In digital recording, the measuring of an electric current, representing an analog sound wave, at different points, in order to build up a digital representation of the wave.

secondary cell (or **accumulator**) An electrochemical cell or battery that can be recharged.

secondary color A color made by mixing two primary colors.

semiconductor A type of material that acts as a conductor or as an insulator, depending on its temperature.

series circuit An electric circuit in which the current passes through the components one after another.

shutter A flap on a camera that controls the length of time light falls on the film.

silicon chip (also **integrated circuit** or **chip**) A tiny piece of silicon with a complete electronic circuit etched onto it.

SI units An internationally agreed system of standard units used for scientific measurement.

solar cell A device that converts the Sun's energy into electricity.

solenoid (or **coil**) A coil of wire that behaves like a magnet when an electric current passes through it.

sonar Echo location when used by ships to detect underwater objects, such as shipwrecks or shoals of fish.

sonic boom A loud bang heard when the built-up, overlapping sound waves (**shock wave**) produced by an aircraft moving at supersonic speed pass a listener.

soundbox A box that resonates and so amplifies the original sound.

sound synthesizer An instrument that stores sound waves as binary code and can reproduce the original sound by converting the code into an electric current and sending it to a speaker.

sound wave (or **acoustic wave**) A longitudinal, mechanical wave that carries sound energy through a medium.

static electricity Electrical charge held by a material.

subsonic speed Any speed below the speed of sound.

subtractive mixing The type of mixing which occurs when pigments are mixed, resulting from some parts of the visible light spectrum being absorbed by pigment while other parts are reflected.

supersonic speed Any speed greater than the speed of sound.

T **erminal** (or **pole**) A point on a source of potential difference, for example a battery, where wires are connected to make an electric circuit.

thermistor A resistor which gives different amounts of resistance, depending on the temperature.

timbre The distinctive sound quality of a musical instrument. The same note played by different instruments sounds different because of their timbre. See also *harmonics*.

transistor An electronic component which acts as a switch by using a small current to control a larger one.

transverse waves Waves in which the vibrations are at right angles to the direction of travel.

turbine A machine with a shaft and blades, which are turned, for example, by the force of wind or steam. The movement energy is converted into electricity.

U **ltrasound** Sound waves with a frequency above 20,000 hertz. The echoes of ultrasound waves are used in **ultrasound scanning** to form a picture of the inside of the body.

ultraviolet radiation (**ultraviolet rays**) Electromagnetic waves that lie just beyond the violet end of the visible light spectrum.

umbra A dark shadow formed where no light reaches an area.

V **ariable resistor** (or **rheostat**) An electronic component that can be adjusted to give different amounts of resistance.

viewfinder The part of a camera that allows the photographer to see what will appear on the picture.

visible light spectrum The narrow section of the electromagnetic spectrum that humans can see. It is made up of red, orange, yellow, green, blue, indigo and violet light.

volt (**V**) The SI unit of potential difference.

voltage See *potential difference*.

voltmeter A device used to measure the potential difference between two points.

W **avelength** The distance between one crest (or trough) of a wave and the next.

X **-rays** Short wavelength, high frequency electromagnetic waves that can pass through most soft substances but not hard, dense ones.

INDEX

You will find the main explanations of terms in the index on the pages shown in bold type. It may be useful to look at the other pages for further information.

See for yourself answers

Page 42

The red (2) red (2) blue (6) silver (±10%) resistor has the highest rating, with a value of between 19,800,000Ω and 24,200,000Ω. The green (5) green (5) black (0) silver (±10%) resistor is worth between 49.5Ω and 60.5Ω.

WEB SITES

ACKNOWLEDGEMENTS

PHOTO CREDITS
(t = top, m = middle, b = bottom, l = left, r = right)

Corbis: **1** Gary Bartholemew; **2-3** <CRDPHOTO>; **4-5** Roger Ressmeyer; **10-11** (b) Peter Johnson; **12-13** (b) George Hall; **20-21** (t) Stuart Westmorland; **21** (br) Charles Michael Murray; **22-23** (t) Joseph Sohm, ChromoSohm Inc; **24-25** (b) Steve Austin, Papillio; **26** (tr) Charles E. Rotkin; **28** (bl) Jamie Harron, Papillio; **34-35** Kennan Ward; **36-37** (b) Peter Hardholdt; **38** (t) The Purcell Team; **40-41** (b) Lowell Georgia; **43** (br) Charles O'Rear

© **Digital Vision**: **8-9** (main); **10** (tr); **13** (tr); **14** (tr), (mr), (bl); **20** (ml); **22** (m); **31** (mr); **39** (tr); **44** (tr); **48** (b); **50** (tr); **51** (tr). **Science Photo Library**: **cover** Colin Cuthbert, Hugh Turvey; **6-7** Adam Hart-Davis; **18** (tr) Hugh Turvey.

Airbus Industrie 48 (tl); **Allsport UK Ltd 33** (tr); **American Government 13** (ml); **Arriflex 31**; **British Telecom 53** (tr); **Dell 46** (m); **Diamond Multimedia 48** (tr); **Epson** Perfection 610 Scanner **49** (l); **Gateway 46** (bl), **49** (t); **Guillemot 49** (ml); **Intel 45** (tr), (ml), **47** (m), (ml); **Microsoft 46** (mr), **49** (bl) (screen shot reprinted with permission from Microsoft Corporation); **Philips 33** (tr), (m); **Sony 31** (bm); **The Royal Festival Hall Gamelan Programme, London 14** (bl); **Charlotte Tomlins 13** (mr); **Two Way TV 33** (tr); **Yamaha-Kemble Music (UK) Ltd 15** (bl); **3Com 51** (ml); **NASA 52**

ILLUSTRATORS
Simone Abel, Sophie Allington, Jane Andrews, Rex Archer, Paul Bambrick, Jeremy Banks, Andrew Beckett, Joyce Bee, Stephen Bennett, Roland Berry, Gary Bines, Isabel Bowring, Trevor Boyer, John Brettoner, Gerry Browne, Peter Bull, Hilary Burn, Andy Burton, Terry Callcut, Kuo Kang Chen, Stephen Conlin, Sydney Cornfield, Dan Courtney, Steve Cross, Gordon Davies, Peter Dennis, Richard Draper, Brin Edwards, John Francis, Mark Franklin, Peter Geissler, Nick Gibbard, William Giles, Mick Gillah, David Goldston, Peter Goodwin, Jeremy Gower, Teri Gower, Terry Hadler, Alan Harris, Nick Hawken, Nicholas Hewetson, Christine Howes, John Hutchinson, Ian Jackson, Hans Jessen, Karen Johnson, Richard Johnson, Elaine Keenan, Aziz Khan, Stephen Kirk, Richard Lewington, Brian Lewis, Jason Lewis, Steve Lings, Rachel Lockwood, Kevin Lyles, Chris Lyon, Kevin Maddison, Janos Marffy, Andy Martin, Josephine Martin, Rob McCaig, Joseph McEwan, David McGrail, Malcolm McGregor, Dee McLean, Annabel Milne, Robert Morton, Paddy Mounter, Louise Nevet, Martin Newton, Louise Nixon, Steve Page, Justine Peek, Maurice Pledger, Mick Posen, Russell Punter, Barry Raynor, Mark Roberts, Michael Roffe, Michelle Ross, Simon Roulstone, Graham Round, Michael Saunders, John Scorey, John Shackell, Chris Shields, David Slinn, Graham Smith, Guy Smith, Peter Stebbing, Ian Stephen, Sue Stitt, Stuart Trotter, Robert Walster, Craig Warwick, Ross Watton, Phil Weare, Hans Wiborg-Jenssen, Sean Wilkinson, Gerald Wood, David Wright, Nigel Wright.

Every effort has been made to trace the copyright holders of the material in this book. If any rights have been omitted, the publishers offer to rectify this in any future edition, following notification. The publishers are grateful to the following organizations and individuals for their contribution and permission to reproduce material. Microsoft® Windows® 95 and Microsoft® Internet Explorer are either registered trademarks or trademarks of Microsoft Corporation in the United States and other countries. Netscape, Netscape Navigator and the N logo are registered trademarks of Netscape Communications Corporation in the United States and other countries. Java and all Java-based trademarks and logos are trademarks or registered trademarks of Sun Microsystems Inc in the United States and other countries.

American editor: Carrie A. Seay

DATE DUE			